can you hear me now?

Also by Dwain Neilson Esmond:
Beyond the In-a-Pinch God

To order, **call 1-800-765-6955**.
Visit us at **www.reviewandherald.com** for information
on other Review and Herald® products.

can you hear me now?

YOUNG ADULT DEVOTIONAL

DWAIN NEILSON ESMOND

REVIEW AND HERALD® PUBLISHING ASSOCIATION
HAGERSTOWN, MD 21740

Copyright © 2004 by
Review and Herald® Publishing Association
All rights reserved

The author assumes full responsibility for the accuracy of all facts and quotations as cited in this book.

Unless otherwise noted, Scripture quotations in this book are from the *Holy Bible, New International Version.* Copyright © 1973, 1978, 1984, International Bible Society. Used by permission of Zondervan Bible Publishers.

Scripture quotations identified CEV are from the Contemporary English Version. Copyright © American Bible Society 1991, 1995. Used by permission.
Bible texts credited to KJV are from the King James Version.
Texts credited to Message are from *The Message.* Copyright © 1993, 1994, 1995, 1996, 2000, 2001, 2002. Used by permission of NavPress Publishing Group.
Scripture quotations marked NASB are from the *New American Standard Bible,* copyright © 1960, 1962, 1963, 1968, 1971, 1972, 1973, 1975, 1977, 1994 by The Lockman Foundation. Used by permission.
Scripture quotations marked NLT are taken from the *Holy Bible,* New Living Translation, copyright © 1996. Used by permission of Tyndale House Publishers, Inc., Wheaton, Illinois 60189. All rights reserved.
Verses marked TLB are taken from *The Living Bible,* copyright © 1971 by Tyndale House Publishers, Wheaton, Ill. Used by permission.

This book was
Edited by Kalie Kelch
Copyedited by James Cavil and Delma Miller
Cover designed by Leumas Design
Interior design by Candy Harvey
Electronic makeup by Shirley M. Bolivar
Cover photo by Getty Images/Peter Sherrard
Typeset: 11/13 Bembo

PRINTED IN U.S.A.

08 07 06 05 04   5 4 3 2 1

R&H Cataloging Service
Esmond, Dwain Neilson, 1971–
    Can you hear me now?

    1. Youth—Prayerbooks and devotions—English.   I. Title

242.63

ISBN 0-8280-1822-7

In praise of Kemba. I like her—a lot.

Contents

INTRODUCTION			9
CHAPTER	1	~ God Is Not . . .	11
CHAPTER	2	~ God Is . . .	26
CHAPTER	3	~ Why God Speaks	39
CHAPTER	4	~ "Don't You Say That!"	53
CHAPTER	5	~ How God Speaks	67
CHAPTER	6	~ Sweet Lips!	81
CHAPTER	7	~ When God Speaks	95
CHAPTER	8	~ Weird Godspeak	108
CHAPTER	9	~ Where God Speaks	121
CHAPTER	10	~ Verbal Assassins	134
CHAPTER	11	~ In God's Presence	148

Introduction

nother book about communication? I pondered that question for some time as I searched for possible topics to write about. Who wants to read another one of those? Devotional books are never easy to write—a truth I'm still learning. However, if there is one issue that has gotten under my skin through my teen years and now young adulthood—it's the challenge of discovering and knowing God's voice.

Ever wonder what God's will for your life is? How about whom to date or marry? Not quite there yet? What about that career you're dreaming about? Need any guidance on that front? If you said yes to any of these questions, then you need to hear God's voice.

I believe most of us yearn for that Enoch experience—walking and talking with God each day (though we try everything else before trying God). What kind of relationship could we have with God that would make Him interrupt earth's cycle of life and death to take us away with Him? That's some kinda cool.

But how do we "hook up" with God like that? Was Enoch just walking along one day and ran into God while He was taking a stroll? What's more, Enoch probably didn't live in the kind of society we live in today, right?

You would probably agree with me that we suffer from a sort of non-spiritual sensory overload. We live in a society in which the average person spends more than 20 hours a week watching television, and that's not counting time spent at school, work, or hanging out with family and friends. We are neck-deep in the information age. Everyone has e-mail, two cell phones, a pager, and a PDA. Yet we're more unfocused than ever before. What's up?

I have a theory on what's up. There is a huge God deficit in our lives.

Maybe you haven't experienced it, but I certainly have. Sometimes I feel as if someone ran off with God and refuses to bring Him back. *Where is God?* my heart screams. *I left Him here just a few short days ago, and now I can't find Him.*

How can we see God through all the clutter in our lives? In this book I try to start at the beginning by defining who God is not. I use a number of high-profile people and illustrations to draw a stark comparison, not so much to denigrate them, but to give the reader a sense of the spiritual distance between God and us. He really is God of the universe. He is the highest order of being there is.

In this book you will learn more about who God is, why and how He speaks, when He chooses to communicate, and how to tune our ears to the beat of heaven. You will understand what it means to hook up with God, to plug in to the awesome Source of all life and wisdom. Tuning in to the frequency of heaven is not like getting cable with a few channels of programming. It's basically getting everything that God is every day. It's a spiritual sensory overload that will change everything about us.

God gives power to live a delivered life, power to touch everyone who comes in contact with you, power to become God's sons and daughters. If you've never talked to God or cannot recognize His voice; if all you hear is silence when you call out to Him, this book is for you.

CHAPTER 1

God Is Not . . .

God Is Not J-Lo

"For I am the Lord, I change not; therefore ye sons of Jacob are not consumed" *(Malachi 3:6, KJV).*

I know what you're thinking right now. *Duh! God is not J-Lo, Mr. Esmond. And by the way, we need to check your credentials to see if you've decided to exercise your citizenship rights for Planet Estupido.* Before you put me out to pasture, just hang in there, if for no other reason than to see me make a total fool of myself. That should be worth at least a laugh or two, right?

That God is not Jennifer Lopez is a safe pronouncement. Such a statement is sure to attract the ire of no one; no congressional bills need be passed to that effect, no stately proclamations necessary.

I've watched with some interest the career of this dancing, singing, acting machine, so ubiquitous that she is known by an abbreviation of her name. She is a marketer's dream—attractive from head to toe, a fairly good singer, and she can shake her rump with the best of them. (Don't ask me how I know.)

I remember when J-Lo was a nameless "fly girl" on *In Living Color,* Fox's long-defunct comedy variety show. Among the many stars born on that show were Jim Carrey, the brothers Wayans, and David Alan Grier, to name a few. J-Lo was nowhere in sight, not even a blip on the radar screen. But oh, what a difference a few years make. Now Jennifer Lopez is a household name, a bankable star with a massive following.

Along with thousands of other Americans, I took some interest in the relationship that blossomed between Lopez and Bad Boy executive Sean

CAN YOU HEAR ME NOW?

Puffy Combs—P Diddy. It was an odd but high-powered pairing, and the tabloids loved it. The headlines read like the title of some raunchy romance novel: "Bad Boy Meets Good Girl" and "Puffy's New Love."

All was great, it seemed, until the night when Combs and Lopez left a Manhattan nightclub amid a hail of bullets, you might recall. Combs was indicted on illegal gun possession charges, and the "clean" reputation of the good girl who made it big was sullied. In what could only be called a New York minute, J-Lo dropped Puffy so hard that he changed his moniker to P Diddy. Of course, the high-profile split sold oodles of magazines and tabloid papers.

If there ever was a time that Puffy Combs needed Ms. Lopez, it was at that moment. His trial was looming, he was facing major jail time, and his music, fashion, and publishing empire was crumbling amid scandal. No more parties with A-List guests like Donald Trump and the infamous Martha Stewart. No more hanging out in the Hamptons. Of course, I don't know what all took place, but it seemed like an odd time to suck the air out of the Puffmeister.

It was scarcely a few months before Lopez was on to bachelor number two—or was it three? I must confess, I don't even know his name. Next came a shotgun wedding to the nameless one, as comedians joked that Mr. Jennifer Lopez was enjoying his honeymoon.

Fast-forward a few months. The new marriage ended almost when it started as J-Lo took a fancy for Mr. Ben Affleck, Matt Damon's twin and "star" of several mediocre flicks.

I guess we shouldn't be surprised by celebrity relationships that blow up overnight and die with a whimper the next morning. If Pamela Anderson can change her last name to Lee, Rock, and who knows what else in the time it takes you to say divorce, why can't Ms. Lopez change men when she's ready?

I shouldn't be too hard on Hollywood's glitterati, because stars are human beings just like you and me, even if they think their perfect tans and beachfront homes somehow elevate them to a higher status. We are all in need of a Savior, right? We all need God.

What unsettles me about the willy-nillyness with which stars—and nonstars—approach relationships is the reality of a God whose commitment to us is so unlike anything we know or see. It wouldn't really matter what people did if we didn't know God. But because we know God, we can't help yearning for people like J-Lo to get to know Him. Why doesn't she try out Bachelor Number Four?

12

God Is Not . . .

We're not sure how tall He is, but we are made in His image, and some say He is altogether lovely. He is king of the universe, and the sky is His floor, heaven His playground.

If she met God, she would find someone who doesn't change, someone whose passionate love would calm a thousand midnights. She would find in Him the love of her life. That's the God who summons you to the throne room of His glory for a little face time, a little one-on-one, a little TLC.

Isn't it time you tasted true commitment?

THE 411. . . . .

In the book of Malachi, God is addressing a fickle people who have spurned His love. It is a gripping little book that you should read. Malachi 3:6 makes it clear that it is God's consistency that keeps us alive. If God's love were fickle, burning hot on some days and cold on others, what do you think would happen to us? Try this activity: Subtract God from your life. Then make a list of what things in your life would change.

God Is Not Michael Jordan

"They were amazed at his teaching because his message had authority" (Luke 4:32).

Before I pan another celebrity, please allow me to make a disclaimer—at least about Michael Jordan. I happen to like Mr. Jordan a lot. I grew up during the Michael Jordan era in basketball. I cut my teeth on *Come Fly With Me,* parts one and two. I saw Michael play live. I sang, "If I could be like Mike," Gatorade's catchy little ditty. On the basketball court he is in a class by himself.

With that said, let the games begin. Ask yourself the following questions: What does Michael Jordan think about the fact that 15-year-olds in the ghetto pay more than $150 for a pair of his sneakers? How does Mr. Jordan feel about the sweatshop conditions in which some of his shoes used to be made? What does Mr. Jordan think about the fact that AIDS is ravaging African countries at a rate that will cause future generations to look back at us and shake their heads? What does Mr. Jordan think? Does he think?

You're talking again, and I can hear you. You're saying, "Deewain, let it go. He's an old school 'playa' just trying to cement his legacy. Must everyone with a stage have a view on every problem in the world?"

Well, you have a point. Mr. Jordan cannot be expected to weigh in

13

CAN YOU HEAR ME NOW?

on every issue that comes up. In fact, Michael Jordan is quite generous with a variety of charities. That's a good thing, and he should be commended for his work.

However, call me needy, because I want more. Every time Mr. Jordan speaks in public it's always about basketball. I guess there wouldn't be a problem with that if life were one endless basketball game, but as we all know, life is much more than that. Real people exist outside the arena, away from America's obsession with its sports stars.

Why don't we demand more of them, such as asking them to use their considerable wealth and presence to bring about change in the way that our government treats such segments of the population as the poor of Appalachia or the destitute in Newark, New Jersey?

Instead of that gray "no comment" we might get a fiery hot determination to leave a legacy beyond that of the greatest player ever to lace up a pair of Nikes.

"Keep dreamin', Dwain. Ain't gonna happen, dude." I hear you mocking my rant.

That's why God isn't Michael Jordan. God gets into the fray. He doesn't disappear when the issues become dicey. He doesn't board His private jet to Bermuda to soothe His troubled mind—mostly because His mind is never troubled, and jets are not His preferred mode of travel. He doesn't duck the spotlight. He is God interactive. He is on the scene, and He's got an opinion.

If Jesus had been worried about His reputation, it would've made sense not to associate with Mary Magdalene. The woman with the issue of blood wouldn't have had a prayer if Jesus had been concerned about how she smelled. Would He really hang out in the home of a vertically challenged tax cheat? No, He wouldn't. But when He spoke, everyone took notice, because He spoke as one who had authority. He was a true believer.

Jesus was unmoved by the press and its misstatements and half-truths. At the height of His fame the Jews wanted to make Jesus king. He could've ridden the wave of popularity straight through the downfall of Rome and the rise of His kingdom. But His mission was otherworldly. He came to seek and to save lost people (Luke 19:10), and no amount of political correctness could deter Him.

This amazing Being wants an audience with you. Can you believe it? He who puts His thoughts and beliefs out where everyone can see them wants to meet you for a drink—of living water. He wants to butt into your life, to have His say as you walk along your journey.

God Is Not . . .

God won't twiddle His thumbs while you take an L in the game of life. His heart breaks at the thought that anyone would lay a finger on you. John, perhaps Jesus' closest disciple, said it this way: "How great is the love the Father has lavished on us, that we should be called children of God! And that is what we are!" (1 John 3:1).

I like my God strong, not watered down. I like my God straight—like drinking a two-liter bottle of ginger ale straight. That's the kind of strong I like. We serve a big-mouth, know-it-all, in-your-face God, and I wouldn't change a thing about Him.

THE 411. . . . .

Sometimes you've got to be heard on the issues of the day. You've got to take a stand, get involved, and be counted. If you care about God's world, you'll do it. If you care about God's people, you'll do it. "Why should I do it?" you ask. Read Romans 15:1-6. What can you do this week to touch a life?

God Is Not a Republicrat

"The law from your mouth is more precious to me than thousands of pieces of silver and gold" (Psalm 119:72).

In case you were wondering what a Republicrat is, it's a Republican who happens to be a Democrat. Still puzzled? You may know his twin, Demopublican. Still confused? Let me explain.

If you're like me, you're up to your ears in politics—or maybe you've totally tuned out the mindless drivel coming from the numerous wannabes vying for the title of public servant. Once they get into office, many will drop the servant from their title, since they will now be serving themselves and their friends.

During election time, candidates go to great pains to point out just how different they are from their competitors. More often than not the process weeds out anyone who is independent or from a third party. He or she might as well be from another planet, because the two dominant parties, Republican and Democrat, have the system rigged to spit out anyone who isn't like one of them. That's how someone like Ralph Nader, a consumer activist with a real record of public service, can be marginalized and forgotten. Did you see him debate George Bush and Al Gore in the 2000 election? I rest my case.

15

Can You Hear Me Now?

The Democrats would like you to believe that they are the party of average Americans. They are the party of the unions, the small guy fighting big corporations, the party that cares about meat-and-potatoes issues.

The Republicans, on the other hand, also claim to be the party of the average Joe. They work to construct a business-friendly government so as to keep the economy sound and the little guy employed. If businesses fail, the little guy loses big-time, so they work hard to take care of the businesses that employ the little guy. This is an oversimplification of both parties, but work with me here.

Are both parties what they claim to be? Not! Democrats, for all their concern about the ordinary people in America, accept monstrous contributions from large corporations who lobby them mercilessly for tax breaks and business-friendly legislation.

A dirty little secret that Democrats don't want us to know is that the foundation for the financial scandals of 2002 (i.e., Enron, WorldCom, Adelphia, Quest, Tyco, Johnson and Johnson, etc.) was laid during the Clinton years when the president's administration looked the other way on pro-business legislation passed by a Republican-controlled Congress. Every one of the bills that would've prevented companies from falsifying information on their quarterly reports never saw the light of a vote in Congress.

The Republicans, for their moralizing and family values, aren't much better. Many of the unethical CEOs they pilloried in the media just a few years ago were close friends of President George W. Bush and the Republican establishment. They gave record sums to the Bush administration. Here's a quick trivia question. How many top-level business executives in George W. Bush's administration? The answer might surprise you: eight—including Bush and Cheney. Can you say big business?

I guess none of this is surprising. Politicians have been misleading the public for years. For all their lofty ideals and "read my lips" promises, they are people just like you and me. They are basically all the same, with few exceptions. Are there honest people in Congress who are trying to do what is right? Absolutely! Are they the majority of politicians? Oh, no.

Whether R or D or I, it really doesn't matter. The answer always ends up being the same: We will do what is best for us, and if there's anything left we'll throw the people a bone or two.

To some this rant will read like the manifesto of some disaffected nonvoter bent on doing nothing. To be honest, it probably is. However, there is some good to the condition of our political system—which remains the best in the world: It makes me long for heaven.

I yearn for some straight talk from folks who aren't corrupted by money or special-interest perks. I want to talk with someone who is ethically bulletproof, whose word is the same yesterday, today, and forever. I believe if Daniel were a senator from Rhode Island, I would be able to trust his word. If Enoch were speaker of the House, no bills hurting the interest of the people would ever make it to the president's desk. Of course, both Enoch and Daniel would be the skunks of Washington, D.C. I think their political careers would end before they ever started.

I should become more politically active, but you know what? I think I'll settle for telling ordinary people about a God who has never lied and isn't planning to anytime soon. I'll tell them to continue working to make their society better one family member, neighbor, friend, and coworker at a time. I'll tell them not to paint everyone with the broad stroke of disdain, as I may have done here. I'll tell them that people can change, but not to be surprised if they don't live to see it.

And I'll tell them to trust in God.

THE 411 . . . .

A wise person once uttered: "You can fool all the people some of the time and some of the people all the time, but you cannot fool all the people all the time." I think that's how it goes. The truth of this statement is echoed in the fact that truth inevitably rises to the surface. Sometimes it takes minutes, sometimes centuries. Read Ecclesiastes 12:13 and 14. What does this tell us about God's sense of right and wrong?

God Is Not Beyoncé or Britney

"The creation waits in eager expectation for the sons of God to be revealed" *(Romans 8:19).*

Sex.

Now that I have your attention, let's talk!

It is one of the most misunderstood words in any language. In most societies the act of copulation is divorced from the act that first occurs in the brain. What do I mean?

Jesus, standing before a multitude sitting along the gentle slopes of a mountainside, had this to say about sex from the neck up: "You have heard that it was said, 'Do not commit adultery.' But I tell you that anyone who looks at a woman lustfully has already committed adultery with her in his

17

CAN YOU HEAR ME NOW?

heart" (Matthew 5:27, 28). Wow, I'm in trouble. All those who have ever committed adultery, please raise your right hand. Let the record show that Mr. Esmond's hand is elevated.

The truth is that we live in a society that is oversexed. Sex sells everything from cars to toothpicks. I was watching a sporting event one Sunday afternoon, only to be interrupted by a quite revealing commercial for, of all things, beer. I thought to myself, *If beer drinkers looked this good, I might be tempted. But that 300-pounder down by the corner—you know, the one with the heart tattooed on his right bicep—ain't cute.* And we won't even mention his "aroma" wafting on the summer zephyrs.

It should come as no surprise then that the music industry would hitch its star to the best bodies they can find, preferably seminude ones. It really doesn't matter if they don't have any talent—all they seem to need is half a personality and some good looks. To be sure, many of them work hard, travel endlessly, and are forced to sacrifice whatever principles they have for the sake of sales, but I'm not going to feel sorry for them as they cruise by in their Bentleys and custom-built Benzes.

Two of the industry's most "sexy" sirens are Britney Spears and Beyoncé Knowles, the latter formerly of Destiny's Child and Austin Powers fame. Their style, though somewhat on the wane now, has spawned an army of half-dressed imitators in painted-on jeans sporting belly buttons that whistle to you no matter what time of the day or season.

Maybe I'm obsessing about a trivial issue, but I don't think so. This soft-core image so forcefully projected by the media changes those who expose themselves to it. The message in the image seems to be "show what your mama gave ya" and you'll get what you want. Boys expect you to show some skin. Girls like to see abs, not flab. How else are you going to get their attention? Even Christian young adults feel the pressure.

But now that you have that honey's digits, what's next? Are you going to give her a Bible study? I don't think so. If undressing is how you get what you want, chances are you want the wrong things.

I have a pet theory, and it goes something like this. When anyone, male or female, has to bare their body to get attention, it's usually a sign that they lack depth on the inside. The more physically revealing a person is, the shallower they tend to be. That's my theory. What do you think? Am I off my rocker?

The Bible speaks of another kind of unveiling, one that actually changes the way we dress on the outside, and guess what? The whole world is waiting to see it. The world is dying to see God's children reveal themselves.

God Is Not . . .

They want a snapshot of what God is like. Who is God? they're asking. What is He like? What do His followers look like? In a culture that cherishes surface beauty at the expense of inner beauty, imagine what a difference a Christian can make.

What would happen if you threw on a humble spirit before you walked out today? What would people think if you painted your lips with the gospel of the soon-coming Savior? What if you dressed in the righteousness of Christ? What would your friends think? What would God think? That's the beauty God wishes to see when He looks at you. Now, that's hot!

Britney Spears and Beyoncé Knowles—and the other stars in the skin trade—are God's children, and He loves them. But make no mistake—He is not them. He loves us, but He is not us.

He cares about everything we are on the inside and everything we wear on the outside. He wants to reveal Himself to us and through us. We are His billboard, His video, His movie, His commercial. He is a God who cares about His image, and we have a lot to do with that.

THE 411. . . . .

Read 1 Peter 3:3 and 4. What point is the apostle Peter trying to make here? Do these verses mean that we shouldn't care about our outward appearance? How can you strike a balance between inward and outward adornment?

God Is Not Hamas

"For his anger lasts only a moment, but his favor lasts a lifetime; weeping may remain for a night, but rejoicing comes in the morning" (Psalm 30:5).

Unless you live on another planet, there's a good chance you've heard of Hamas, the radical Palestinian terrorist organization currently waging war against Israel for the liberation of Palestine. On this Sunday morning I turned on the TV to find that there had just been another terrorist suicide bombing in Israel. The news cameras panned to the shredded hull of a bus. The roof had been torn off, and some of the seats lay outside the windows.

The bus was a terrifying sight of twisted metal and fiberglass. Ambulances dashed about the scene, followed by packs of emergency personnel who looked lost. The ones who had been injured were carted off to hospital emergency rooms as the people of Israel and Palestine

CAN YOU HEAR ME NOW?

added one more gruesome tale to their grotesque battle.

Hamas, I would later find out, bombed the bus in retaliation for the Israeli military's killing of a local Hamas leader. Incidentally, the Israeli armed forces attempted to execute the Hamas leader from thousands of feet in the air—not the best way to kill one person. The air strike killed not only the target but also several women and children. Hamas vowed revenge for the attack. A few weeks later Hamas bombed a university in Israel, killing and injuring several, including five Americans. And then there was today's attack.

The reality of this type of aggression has become so commonplace that I struggle to summon the sense of horror that used to grip me when I first saw such crimes. I must confess: I can't really wrap my mind around such rage. In my former life, before Christ, I was known as something of a hothead—but I can scarcely conjure this brand of anger, one that burns for decades. I guess I simply haven't been hurt bad enough.

Today we live in a world where people are giving up on diplomacy. If you doubt that, consider Operation Iraqi Freedom, championed by President George W. Bush. Remember, he took us to war based on flimsy evidence of Saddam Hussein's weapons of mass destruction. It turns out, as we now know, that the U.N. weapons inspectors had done a very good job of disarming Mr. Hussein. I shudder to think that so many people died for a cause that made no sense.

No one wants to talk things through anymore. Every slight is a challenge to one's sense of self. "If I don't stand up to this clown on the playground, then I might as well stay in bed for the next nine months and never go to school," some of my younger friends say.

If you get into a fender bender with another motorist, you have to be worried about being dragged from your car and beaten to death, like the motorist and his passenger who were killed by onlookers when their vehicle jumped the curb and hit several people in a Chicago suburb. Blood was everywhere that day, staining the sidewalk and flowing into the street. It was such a freakish event that normally loquacious reporters and commentators were at a loss for words to describe the incident.

People today are feeling powerless to affect situations that touch their lives. You really can't afford to drop out of school today, not when recent studies show that the gap in pay between those with only a high school diploma and those with a college degree is around $20,000 and climbing. The challenge of buying a new home or caring for a growing family forces many parents to work two and three jobs. When these people leave work,

God Is Not . . .

they're tired, stressed out, and often angry. This anger is expressed in spousal and child abuse, workplace violence, etc.

Once when I got angry at something a coworker had done, I barged into his office and almost cleaned the floor with him. It wasn't one of my better moments. Later I had to beg God's forgiveness and his. I had no idea that I was so keyed up. It just all bubbled to the surface in one big volcanic eruption that everyone in the department could hear. Can you say embarrassed?

In a world gone mad it's good to know that God is not like us. He is not Hamas, the Israeli military, the doofus in your high school slapping you around every day, or you—the one plotting to take care of that jerk once and for all. God is not the mob that beat the motorist and his passenger to death on the sidewalk.

When God gets angry it's usually for good reason, and even then when He expresses His anger it is calculated to bring about positive change. But what about the countless innocents in the Bible slain at the request of God? I must admit that I struggle with this issue probably more than any other in the Bible. Many times God's judgment came after much pleading and warning. At other times God simply withdrew His protection from His people so they could be boss of their own lives, determiner of their own destiny. Needless to say, they usually wanted Him back in charge. Just read the book of Judges.

I'm so thankful that God doesn't retain His anger forever. He gets mad, He gets active, and then He gives all of heaven to get us back into the fold.

No, the God we serve is not like Hamas. The end of His displeasure is love.

THE 411. . . . .

Think of some of the recent incidents of crime and violence you have heard about. Do you sometimes wonder if God is taking note of all the evil deeds happening around the world? Read Psalm 103:6. How does God work righteousness and justice for all the oppressed?

God Is Not Enron

"My whole being will exclaim, 'Who is like you, O Lord? You rescue the poor from those too strong for them, the poor and needy from those who rob them'" (Psalm 35:10).

21

Can You Hear Me Now?

Remember Enron? By now the furor over the failed energy trader has subsided somewhat. How about WorldCom, Quest, Global Crossing, Adelphia, Tyco? Do you remember them? What do they all have in common? Each of these companies defrauded thousands of investors and employees of their firms.

Basically the scheme worked this way. Investors would invest money in these companies, sometimes on a weekly or monthly basis. Then the CEOs, CFOs, COOs, and other company execs would construct elaborate loans for themselves. Bernie Ebbers, former CEO of WorldCom, was given a $400 million loan, even as accountants were incorrectly stating the true worth of the company's stock. It's like putting your money in a piggy bank, only to have your big brother, already rich and increased with goods, steal it whenever he wanted to.

Some investors worked more than 40 years to put away a little nest egg, some peace of mind at the end of life. They weren't rich by any stretch, just enough to live comfortably until the inevitable happened. In some cases hundreds of thousands of dollars were reduced to pennies when stock values plunged. In the late nineties and early on in the twenty-first century we saw greed run amok. CEOs were being compensated at a rate 500 times that of the average employee. For every dollar an employee earned, the CEO of the company received $500.

The government's watchdog for this brand of criminality is the Securities and Exchange Commission (SEC). Unfortunately, it failed. The audit firms charged with making sure that companies obeyed the letter and spirit of the accounting laws were taking money from the big companies to look the other way. The politicians who are now walking around like peacocks touting their record on corporate crime are the same politicians who took the big business money and weakened the SEC so that it could not actively crack down on corporate fraud. And who pays for the Enrons and the WorldComs? You guessed it. We do.

That's a small comfort to the newly destitute that must now go back to work to make ends meet. Some will be forced to flip burgers at McDonald's or greet patrons as they enter Wal-Mart. Hardly the retirement they had in mind.

The greedy don't get off scot-free either. There's a special disease that seems to infect those who make money their god—they're never satisfied. They contract a sort of "getting-itis" that makes life, well, tiring.

No less an authority on the matter, King Solomon spoke of the way the illness takes over the life. "Whoever loves money never has money

God Is Not . . .

enough; whoever loves wealth is never satisfied with his income. This too is meaningless" (Ecclesiastes 5:10). The CEO of Adelphia and his two sons must have been infected; how else can we explain the fact that three men pilfered more than $2.3 billion from their company? What does one do with $2.3 billion?

But Solomon doesn't stop there. He adds a bit of information sure to unsettle the most moneygrubbing capitalist. "As goods increase, so do those who consume them. And what benefit are they to the owner except to feast his eyes on them?" (verse 11). How sad!

I have a picture of God as He watches the exploitation of the poor, the destitute, and the powerless at the hands of the rich and powerful. I see a frown begin to crease His holy brow. I see tears flow down His cheeks. I see the angels record the evil deed with "terrible exactness" in the book of remembrance. I see the heart of God break as He lowers His head. "How could one creature do this to another?" He seems to say. The angels tremble as He pleads for mercy on behalf of the corporate oppressors. At the sight of His Son, God is pleased and extends more grace. He dispatches a retinue of angels to draw close to His loved ones—the oppressed and their oppressors.

No, God is not Enron. His desire is not to exploit you for His own personal benefit. He derives no pleasure from cars, boats, and houses. God jumps for joy when we praise and worship Him. The divine pulse quickens with each prayer, each tear, and each act of contrition. These things please God. When you repent of your sins, heaven breaks out in a fit of celebration and praise (Luke 15:7).

Let the party begin.

THE 411. . . . .
Have you been infected by the greed so commonly seen in our society? Would you be willing to let God show you if you have? Pray this prayer found in Psalm 139:23 and 24.

God Is Not Like Us

" 'For my thoughts are not your thoughts, neither are your ways my ways,' declares the Lord" (Isaiah 55:8).

God is a unique being. Wouldn't you agree? Think about it for a moment. We've never seen Him, but His touch is unmistakable. Like the

23

Can You Hear Me Now?

breeze that blows and no one can really tell where it comes from or where it is going, God moves in the ethereal mist. We know Him from evidences of His presence. To be sure, no one has ever seen the wind, yet we feel it on our skin, we see it move the trees, we watch an eagle ride its gusts, and when it turns destructive we see it reduce a town to rubble.

God makes Himself known in similar ways. How else can we explain the fact that our world sits 93 million miles away from the sun, yet it is heated and cooled at temperatures that make life possible? If the earth somehow slipped just slightly off its axis, we would either burn or freeze to death.

Among the final plagues preceding the judgment, John the revelator mentions the sun burning with "fervent" heat. To achieve this, God doesn't have to turn up the temperature of the sun. Each day as we deplete the ozone layer, the bubble protecting us from the sun's damaging rays, we increase the temperature. He need only leave us to ourselves.

While we share the image of God and are made in His likeness, as we have been learning this week, He is not like us. God's ways surpass our ways. He is at once accessible and untouchable. He is both near and far at the same time. The Creator who strings the galaxies together is an infinite being. He doesn't operate in time; He works through time. Earth's time and scale is but a pause in eternity. God is higher than we are, better than we will ever be, and guess what? He wants us to be like Him. Notice, not to be Him; to be like Him.

The prophet Isaiah gives us a brief glimpse of just how elevated our God is. "Seek the Lord while he may be found; call on him while he is near. Let the wicked forsake his way and the evil man his thoughts. Let him turn to the Lord, and he will have mercy on him, and to our God, for he will freely pardon" (Isaiah 55:6, 7).

At this point God grabs the microphone from Isaiah and begins to explain exactly why we ought to forsake our way and come to Him: " 'For my thoughts are not your thoughts, neither are your ways my ways,' declares the Lord. 'As the heavens are higher than the earth, so are my ways higher than your ways and my thoughts than your thoughts.

" 'As the rain and the snow come down from heaven, and do not return to it without watering the earth and making it bud and flourish, so that it yields seed for the sower and bread for the eater, so is my word that goes out from my mouth: It will not return to me empty, but will accomplish what I desire and achieve the purpose for which I sent it' " (verses 8-11).

Beginning in verse 12 God tells of the blessings that will attend those who plug in to Him and do what He says. The language here is simply

God Is Not . . .

sublime. In poetic tones God speaks of nature receiving us again into the fellowship of obedience to God. Ironically, as bright, intellectual humans, we are the only part of God's creation that knowingly goes against His will. The whole creation is waiting for us, God's special beings, to get our act together.

"'You will go out in joy and be led forth in peace; the mountains and hills will burst into song before you, and all the trees of the field will clap their hands. Instead of the thornbush will grow the pine tree, and instead of briers the myrtle will grow. This will be for the Lord's renown, for an everlasting sign, which will not be destroyed'" (verses 12, 13).

THE 411. . . . .

Do you ever try to play God? In what ways might you be making a god of yourself? Who alone is qualified to be God? Read 1 Chronicles 29:12.

25

CHAPTER 2

God Is . . .

God Is: Creator

"In the beginning God created the heavens and the earth" (Genesis 1:1).

There's always someone willing to take credit for something they had little or nothing to do with. When the economic boom of the late 1990s grew millionaires like weeds after a good rain, President Clinton—and the Republican-led Congress, for that matter—prided themselves on the fact that they had constructed just the right fiscal balance to bring about wealth and success.

However, the boom led to the bust of the early twenty-first century, and corporate greed was paraded for the world to see. No one wanted to claim the credit for that. Success has many fathers, but failure is always a bastard. No one wants to attribute his or her last name to failure.

But let's face it: politicians have no lock on siphoning praise. One of the jobs I had as a kid was sweeping and cleaning a local dentist's office and the tiny walkway that led to the building. I fancied myself on the road to a career in dentistry. (Yeah, right!) Fairly soon the truth became all too clear. I barely saw the customers, let alone getting close to their mouths, which, as it turned out, was a good thing.

I worked with another young friend of mine who was slightly more loquacious than I was. OK, he was a motormouth, and a big one at that. He was frighteningly adept at talking instead of working. I was no slouch in that department either, but I did have a fairly good work ethic, seeing that this was my first "big gig." I was getting paid $15 a week, and that was big money. You could buy about a thousand Now or Later candies for

26

God Is . . .

that. It was cold, hard cash, greenbacks, dinero, moolah, smackaroos, benjamins, coin. It was money, and I was seriously diggin' loot at that age.

One day as I walked into the dentist's office to be paid after a long, hard two-hour workday, I overheard what sounded like a great sucking sound. Timothy, the aforementioned mouth-almighty, tongue-everlasting, was chatting up the dentist. "Well, Mr. Thauborne, I finished cleaning up the front yard. I swept the driveway and removed the rocks. It's all done."

Needless to say, blood began to surge through my brain like the waters of Niagara Falls going through a two-inch pipe. I had to pause to check to see if my ears had deceived me—they had in the past. Tim wasn't just lying; he had doused the dastardly tale with extra mustard, ketchup, oregano, two all-beef patties, special sauce, lettuce, cheese, pickles, onions on a sesame-seed bun. It was a Big Mac-sized lie.

The truth is he didn't do much of the work at all; I did. He did keep me entertained while "we" worked, but he wasn't the foreman overseeing the cleanup of some demolished skyscraper. We were cleaning a yard, for crying out loud.

When I ambled into the office to be paid, Mr. Thauborne was less than enthusiastic. "Esmond, you need to step it up. You're too lazy," he muttered under his breath as he reached for his wallet. *It's over now,* I thought. *He used the L word on me. I'm going to have to key Mr. T's car real good, or at least make a voodoo doll of him and stick it with a thousand pins. It's a toss-up.*

"Well," Tim interrupted shyly as he avoided eye contact with me, "he's a hard worker, Mr. T." He was attempting to return some of the dignity he had stolen from me just a few moments before. I wasn't biting. I took my money and walked out, since it made no sense to clear my name right then. This was a tough crowd. Tim stayed a little while longer to finish the suck-up job I had so rudely interrupted. (I later decided I had better not touch Mr. Thauborne's ride; no need to bite the hand that fed me—you understand.)

Unlike people who misappropriate praise (see *Webster's* under "Tim"), God really did create this planet and the multiplied billions of universes we have yet to discover. It's ludicrous to think that someone would try to knock God off His perch as Creator of the universe.

Saying that our world spontaneously popped into being is like saying there was an explosion at a printshop and out popped *Webster's Unabridged Dictionary,* says one scientist. Another puts it this way: It's like someone taking a running start and jumping over the Empire State Building. Not even LeBron James has hops like that.

CAN YOU HEAR ME NOW?

To understand God's voice, we must accept certain things about Him. The most important thing to accept is that this earth and all its creations belong to God. As my island friends say: "A-He run tings."

This is my Father's world. This is your Father's world. Believe it.

THE 411. . . . .

Read the following verses carefully: Nehemiah 9:6, Job 27:6, Psalm 102:25, Hebrews 11:3. Is it possible that parts of evolutionary theory could work simultaneously with the biblical account of the earth's origins? Is it possible that the effects of sin and its consequences could bring about changes in our world and its inhabitants?

God Is: Life

"Jesus said to her, 'I am the resurrection and the life. He who believes in me will live, even though he dies'" (John 11:25).

A few years ago a movie called *Philadelphia* caught the attention of the public. Tom Hanks and Denzel Washington, two of the highest paid actors on Hollywood's A List, starred in the film. Hanks plays a gay lawyer at a prestigious law firm who contracts AIDS and tries to hide it. Washington enters the movie later as a brash, streetwise esquire, who, you guessed it, happens to be homophobic. He represents Hanks, who is fired when the old bluebloods at the firm find out that one of their shining stars is gay. Sounds plausible.

In one particularly memorable scene Hanks invites Washington to his home after a long day of legal wrangling. Hanks's character is now dying from full-blown AIDS; the lesions are all over his body. Washington, already uneasy about being in the same room with a gay man, listens as Hanks, an opera buff, plays one of his favorite arias.

The soprano, with a voice that could wake the dead, sings to a hopelessly dying man. I must confess, I don't remember much of what she says in the song. (Italian is not my native tongue.) But I do remember the climax of the aria in which she sings with all the gusto she could muster: "I AM LIFE! I AM LIFE!"

This is the most powerful scene in the movie for many reasons. The camera circles Hanks as he translates the words for Washington. His eyes are closed, his head lifted, as the tears begin an eerie race down his cheeks. Washington is uncomfortable with the display of raw emotion, but he is

28

God Is . . .

transfixed. He is moved by Hanks's pain. (He never knew that gay people had feelings.)

After the song ends, a visibly shaken Washington scampers out of the apartment and goes home to his sleeping wife and child. He hugs them tightly.

John, the disciple Jesus loved and was closest to, knew a little something about life and death. He writes his Gospel from a unique perspective. John wants the reader to know that Jesus was God in the flesh, God with all the trimmings. For this reason he chooses just the right mix of miracles to highlight the deity of Christ. John 11 recounts one such episode. You know it well—even if you may have never read it.

A pall had settled over the home of Mary and Martha. Their brother, Lazarus, had now been dead for four days. Any hope of him awakening from a coma was gone. To make matters worse, Jesus, the one person they knew who could scare death off, refused to rush to the scene. He took His sweet time, arriving as the paid mourners were in full wail.

Mary and Martha were enraged. "If you had been here he wouldn't have died," they shrieked through sobs of pain. Their visible disappointment broke the heart of Jesus, and John captures one of the few moments in Scripture when "Jesus wept."

Jesus responds in a curious way: "Your brother will rise again" (John 11:23). "Yeah, right," Martha quips. "Maybe in the resurrection, but he ain't gettin' up anytime soon." I imagine that's when Jesus put His arms around Martha. I believe He pulled her close and whispered in her ear: "Guess what, Martha—I am the resurrection. I AM LIFE." He follows this up with a display of otherworldly power.

"Where did you lay him? Show Me where the tomb is," He said. When He gets there, He asks that the stone blocking the entrance to Lazarus' tomb be removed. Jesus never doubted His Father's power, and after He thanked Him publicly for hearing His prayer, He shouted: "Yo, Laz, where you at?" (OK, those weren't His exact words, but you get the picture.)

The paid mourners stopped their crocodile tears. Life had stared death in the face—and death blinked. On this day death slinked away from the presence of Life a defeated foe as Lazarus walked out to meet his family.

Jesus is life. God is life. There isn't any life apart from *the* Life. Anyone who fails to believe this truth is dying a slow death.

THE 411. . . . .

Read John 5:24. Get a piece of paper and a pen or pencil. Write a paragraph explaining what John means when he says that he who believes Christ's words has passed from death to life. Don't you want to see what it's like on the other side, on the side of life?

God Is: Perfect

"But when perfection comes, the imperfect disappears" (1 Corinthians 13:10).

There are moments in our lives when we must radically adjust our notions and preconceptions. For instance, it really doesn't matter how much you try to sympathize with a girlfriend whose beau just broke her heart. Only when your heart has been broken can you truly empathize. Agree?

Read all the child-rearing books you choose. However, there's nothing quite as mind-altering as a screaming 2-year-old at 3:00 a.m. I don't know from experience, but so I've been told. And hopefully (message to the wife) I'll find out one day soon.

It's the kind of feeling you get watching Tiger Woods win seven out of 12 major championships; watching Venus and Serena Williams devour women's tennis; celebrating with a cancer-free Lance Armstrong as he wins the Tour de France for the umpteenth time. It's like putting up one of my watercolor paintings for auction—and I don't paint—alongside a Picasso or a Monet. It's the difference between night and day.

That's not even a fraction of how much more perfect God is than we are. Think about it for a moment. He makes no mistakes, He never has a dirty thought, He never lies, and He never curses—although He does pronounce curses. He is never afraid, never tired, never sick, and never thirsty—except for the blessing of our companionship. He's perfection on steroids, the absence of all darkness. That's the kinda God I wanna be down with!

He's better than I am, and I like it that way. I'm not God, no matter how many crystal balls I gaze into or how much yoga and meditation I do. It doesn't matter if a million gurus say so; I ain't God. Out of the same mouth with which I bless Him, I curse others. Out of the same heart with which I pronounce undying devotion to Him, I lust after God's hallowed creations. Trust me, it may come as a surprise to you, but I'm not God.

The apostle Paul writes to the Corinthians, and he seems to say to them, "Just wait till you see Him. Wait till you see perfection. No, not the kind that was made flesh and dwelt among us. Wait till you see God the Father, Jesus, and the Holy Spirit as They truly are in Their glorified state.

God Is . . .

Just wait till you get an eyeful of that." Paul says that it's so mind-numbing that all imperfection will cease to be. Things are gonna be a-changin' on that day. You better believe it!

Disease will no longer be—that's great news for the continent of Africa, where AIDS has reduced the life expectancy of an adult to 35 years. Corruption will no longer be a problem—that's bad news for a large number of CEOs. Every need will be supplied in God—that's spectacular news for those who work in the "shadow economy"—pimps and prostitutes, drug dealers and hustlers, the downtrodden and the forgotten, the homeless and the destitute.

Tears will be wiped away—that's hope for the mother and father whose son OD'd on life and decided to end it all. When Perfection comes, like a cosmic Santa He will bring a billion remedies in His sleigh. And there's one especially designed for the hurts that have caused you pain.

When Perfection comes, those who have accepted Jesus Christ as Savior and Lord of their life will be changed. To hear God clearly, you must believe in the infallibility of His voice, thundering from the heavens, even as it whispers in your ear.

He makes no mistakes, my friend. He's perfection with the big P, and that's great news for you and me.

The 411. . . . .

Read Psalm 18:1-30, paying special attention to verse 30. This is a psalm written by King David after God had delivered him from all his enemies, chiefly Saul. It is a psalm of praise, of triumph. But David wasn't always so "high" on God. Read Psalm 10. Is God perfect at all times, or do we sometimes doubt Him?

God Is: Love

"Yet it was the Lord's will to crush him and cause him to suffer" (Isaiah 53:10).

Few chapters of the Bible capture my imagination the way Isaiah 53 does. It predates the birth of Jesus Christ, yet Isaiah outlines in vivid, sometimes gruesome detail the final scenes of Jesus' life, scenes that would not play out for centuries. Amazingly, Jesus, during His ministry on earth, would go to the Temple each Sabbath to read the scrolls, among which were Isaiah's writings. I wonder if Jesus ever read this passage. And if so,

CAN YOU HEAR ME NOW?

how did it make Him feel? Did He recognize that He would suffer this tragic death? I believe He did.

Isaiah 53 tells of a love that exceeds anything on earth. There simply is no greater expression of love than one friend laying down their life for another (John 15:13). I've had to make many sacrifices for others, but nothing close to this. I've lent friends money when they needed it, cried with others when someone they loved died, and stayed up all night when they were afraid. And many have done the same for me.

But none of my friends has ever said, "Yo, D-money, I just shot a guy on Twentieth Street, and the cops are looking for the shooter. You mind going down to the police station and taking the rap? I really need a savior right now. You'll probably get the death penalty, since the person I killed was a federal agent. Are you available to die for me?"

Chances are you've never had a request like that either. Yet that's the situation in which Jesus found Himself. What's more, the vast majority of people for whom He was whipped, castigated, and crucified claim no special relationship with Him. In fact, most can be placed in the pile marked "Enemies of Christ," and are proud of it.

In spite of these facts, it "pleased" the Lord to crush Him for us, to snuff out His life, to asphyxiate Jesus for people who have no desire to accept His sacrifice or His love.

A few years ago in Nigeria the Muslim authorities that controlled segments of the government passed a strict form of Islamic law that, among other things, provides for the stoning of any woman who commits adultery. However, it says nothing about the man who helped her sin. The law doesn't give an "out" to women who may have been raped. If the woman was in any way involved in the act she must be stoned, even if the very man with whom she slept reports her. Crazy, you say?

I believe that Jesus coming to our world to die for sins He never committed is a thousand times worse than the fate facing Nigerian women caught in adultery. For Jesus was not only innocent; He was sinless. There's an ocean of difference between innocence and sinlessness. I could be acquitted of murder and still be held guilty by God for failing to help my neighbor get to know Him. Being innocent of one crime does not make me sinless.

Sinlessness is the highest degree of innocence. Yet for you and me Jesus jumped at the chance to die that we might be saved. His sinless life covered our sinful lives.

Just in case we ever fall, just in the event we ever mess up, just on the off chance that we make a mistake, a pristine life is on the books, ready to be sub-

God Is . . .

stituted for ours. "For God did not send his Son into the world to condemn the world, but to save the world through him" (John 3:17). Praise God!

You need not die for your own sins. He already did. That kind of love demands a response from you and me. What will yours be?

THE 411. . . . .

Read Isaiah 53. Consider closely verses 3–8. What do these verses mean to you? If you could say something to Jesus about His sacrifice for you, what would it be?

God Is: Hope

"Why are you downcast, O my soul? Why so disturbed within me? Put your hope in God, for I will yet praise him, my Savior and my God" (Psalm 42:5).

Ever feel as if the whole world were having a party and someone forgot to invite you? All around you your "road dawgs," family members, relatives, and coworkers were all "gettin' down" while you were on the outside looking in. The sun was shining on everyone else, but you were encased in a bubble darker than a thousand midnights. That's never happened to you, right? Me neither.

On second thought, let me tell you the truth before this book ends right here with a GPS-targeted bolt from you know where. There have been a few times when the world was "jammin'" without me.

I remember trying to break a really bad habit, only to fall again and again and again and again. Did I say again? I read the Bible, scouring its pages for encouraging scriptures, some magic bullet that would render my sin powerless. For a while nothing was working.

I was the only person on the planet suffering. The anthem of my life was a death dirge, sung by a raven at midnight. I felt as if God had had enough of my "never agains."

In my despair I contemplated suicide. Maybe if I wasn't here anymore I could find some peace. That didn't last too long, though, especially when I looked at my precious jewel, Kemba, God's special gift to me. I couldn't leave her.

What would she think if the man who worships the ground she walks on suddenly decided that life wasn't worth living? What would God think? In effect, I would be saying that God didn't have the power to help me win my battle. Suicide was a bad idea, so it had to go.

Can You Hear Me Now?

That's when I decided to give God one more try. I looked at myself in the mirror and said, "You no longer own your will. Hand it over to God. Both of us [me and the man in the mirror] will now take orders from Him. We cannot be trusted to make the right decisions; is that clear?

"Look at us. We're a pretty sorry excuse for Christians. Everything we tried has gone up in smoke. Let's face it: we're just no good at this salvation thing." I'm glad Kemba didn't walk in on me at that moment. I could hear her laugh, "Dwain, are you talking to yourself again?"

It may sound strange, but it's good to unzip your head and let the real you slip out for a moment. (Don't take this too far, however.) Sometimes you've got to do a little "self-speak." Don't worry; you're not crazy—at least not yet.

There is even precedent in the Bible for the mano a mano discourses. The psalmist David, for instance, was known to "encourage" himself in the Lord. To this day no one would accuse him of having a loose noodle upstairs. When he felt like giving up, he would write a song to the Lord. Some were songs of praise; others were songs of despair. Consider this song he composed for the "director of music" found in Psalm 42.

"These things I remember as I pour out my soul: how I used to go with the multitude, leading the procession to the house of God, with shouts of joy and thanksgiving among the festive throng" (verse 4). Sounds like you after a Holy Ghost-filled worship experience, doesn't it?

Here is where the self-chatter begins (quite abruptly, I might add): "Why are you downcast, O my soul? Why so disturbed within me? Put your hope in God, for I will yet praise him, my Savior and my God. My soul is yet downcast within me; therefore I will remember you from the land of the Jordan, the heights of Hermon—from Mount Mizar" (verses 5, 6).

A little self-talk goes a long way. King David was able to speak hope into his life when he took stock of where he was, and when he turned over his powerlessness to God.

Life is difficult. No. Life is downright ugly sometimes. A songwriter once made Longfellow's, "Into each life some rain must fall" part of their composition. They were right. But they didn't stop there. "But after the rain new strength you'll gain," the song continues.

Life's challenges are the soil in which faith grows. It is when God seems farthest away that He is closest to us. The great apostle Paul knew a thing or two about discouragement and despair. He too suffered with a problem he wished God would take from him. We find his story in 2 Corinthians 12:1-10.

God Is . . .

He notes: "Three times I pleaded with the Lord to take it away from me. But he said to me, 'My grace is sufficient for you, my power is made perfect in weakness'" (verses 8, 9). It's good to know that my weaknesses do not scare God off.

If I have God, I have hope!

THE 411. . . . .

What challenges do you face in your life? Get a pen and paper and make a list of the five things that discourage you the most. Then read Isaiah 43:1-3. What do these verses say about God's concern for the challenges you face? Ask God to take away your discouragement and give you hope.

God Is: Alive

"So Peter and the other disciple started for the tomb. Both were running, but the other disciple outran Peter and reached the tomb first" (John 20:3, 4).

Lynching.

The word seems almost out of place, the relic of a bygone era we wish to forget. Imagine looking at a White woman—or worse, saying something to her—and a few moments later having your hands tied behind your back and a rope tied around your neck. Imagine the sheer fright that would grip you as the mob begins to tie the rope to a tree. You hear the taunts, the jeers, the swearing. You look around to see men and women, boys and girls, transformed into demonic agents bent on killing you.

The rope becomes taut as the angry men begin pulling it from the other side, hoisting you into the air. The rope bruises your neck as it slides up and nestles just below your chin. Your breathing is constricted. You are breathless. Your feet do an eerie dance in the air as you struggle for a foundation from which to gain lift. There is none. You are dying and the crowd is cheering, along with the demons from the serpent's lair. As each moment passes they grow quieter and quieter until you hear them no more. Your toes give one final wave to the mob. You are dead.

A photographer with a crude old camera sidles up beside you. He anchors his camera, sticks his head under the black cloth at the back of the camera, and proceeds to take a picture of you. He gets just the right one, the one with your eyes bulging and blood oozing from your beaten face. "This picture will be a collector's item," he intones.

It will adorn a postcard, which will be sold in stores, sent from family

35

CAN YOU HEAR ME NOW?

to family, passed down from generation to generation—a memento of the day the crowd made sure you never looked at a White woman again.

It's now early on a quiet Sunday morning. The crowds that bivouacked endlessly on Friday night were now lazily awaking to the reality that they had killed the "King of the Jews." The fervor that animated them on Friday evening slowly ebbed on Saturday as the reality of their actions set in. This was no ordinary lynching, and they knew it.

Maybe it was the violent storm that enveloped the surrounding countryside that Friday evening. The sky was dark and foreboding, belching its displeasure at the treatment of its Maker. The ground shook with disdain; a mighty quake of resentment vibrated through the mob.

Amid the din some could make out heavenly spectators just behind the clouds. Some silently coddled the notion that this quite possibly was the Son of God, and that thought had slowly begun to eat a hole in their brain. No, this was no ordinary, run-of-the-mill lynching; this was different.

The disciples hid from the mob lest they too should share the fate of their Master. A cold silence permeated what once was a happy group. None of them slept on Friday night, Peter least of all. It was his public disavowal of Christ that silenced him. The others were never questioned about their affiliation with Christ, because they had deserted Him long before the Roman soldiers got to Gethsemane.

They were together on Sunday evening, having ventured briefly on Sunday morning to get some food supplies and to see if anything was stirring. A sense of anticipation gripped them as Peter and John told of the empty tomb. Thomas was incredulous. "You two need to be quiet. There's no need to get people's hopes up. He's dead, and ain't nothin' gonna change that." That's when it happened.

"On the evening of that first day of the week, when the disciples were together, with the doors locked for fear of the Jews, Jesus came and stood among them and said, 'Peace be with you!' After he said this, he showed them his hands and side. The disciples were overjoyed when they saw the Lord" (John 20:19, 20).

Your God and my God cheated death. He is alive and well.

THE 411. . . . .

What does the fact that Jesus rose from the dead mean to you? What if Jesus hadn't risen from the dead? What effect would that have on God's plan to save us from the power of sin? Read 1 Corinthians 15:1-22.

36

God Is . . .

God Is: Redeemer

"You see, at just the right time, when we were still powerless, Christ died for the ungodly" (Romans 5:6).

As I sit to write this entry, a saga has been playing in a rural mining community in Pennsylvania. Three days ago nine miners became trapped more than 200 feet below the earth's surface. Their families were forced to endure the excruciating wait for the equipment needed to tunnel down to the dwindling pocket of air where the men were.

The rescuers were very optimistic as the digging began. Just a few hours, and they would be down to where the men were. But something else went wrong. The bit used on the drill to burrow through the earth broke. This mishap delayed the rescue effort for more than 12 hours. With each passing minute the families grew more frantic.

Ministers were dispatched to the site to keep the families and workers hopeful and calm. It worked. Early in the morning some three and a half days later, rescuers made their way to the men. All nine were alive. All were in good shape, minus a few pounds and some tears. The whole nation exulted at their rescue. It was one of those rare moments when CNN, Fox News, and MSNBC carried good news.

The situation in which the miners found themselves that night is not unlike ours. We too are trapped here in a foreign place, far from our home. What's more, we each share a problem that is slowly killing us—as surely as the miners' oxygen decreased with each passing breath. But that problem has been solved. In his letter to the church in Rome, Paul writes about it.

"Therefore, since we have been justified through faith, we have peace with God through our Lord Jesus Christ, through whom we have gained access by faith into this grace in which we now stand. And we rejoice in the hope of the glory of God. Not only so, but we also rejoice in our sufferings, because we know that suffering produces perseverance; perseverance, character; and character, hope.

"And hope does not disappoint us, because God has poured out his love into our hearts by the Holy Spirit, whom he has given us. You see, at just the right time, when we were still powerless, Christ died for the ungodly. Very rarely will anyone die for a righteous man, though for a good man someone might possibly dare to die. But God demonstrates his own love for us in this: While we were still sinners, Christ died for us.

"Since we have now been justified by his blood, how much more shall we be saved from God's wrath through him! For if, when we were God's

CAN YOU HEAR ME NOW?

enemies, we were reconciled to him through the death of his Son, how much more, having been reconciled, shall we be saved through his life! Not only is this so, but we also rejoice in God through our Lord Jesus Christ, through whom we have now received reconciliation.

"Therefore, just as sin entered the world through one man, and death through sin, and in this way death came to all men, because all sinned— for before the law was given, sin was in the world. But sin is not taken into account when there is no law. Nevertheless, death reigned from the time of Adam to the time of Moses, even over those who did not sin by breaking a command, as did Adam, who was a pattern of the one to come" (Romans 5:1-14).

"Consequently, just as the result of one trespass was condemnation for all men, so also the result of one act of righteousness was justification that brings life for all men" (verse 18).

THE 411. . . . .

God, through Christ, redeemed us and bought us back from Satan's grasp. However, this means nothing if we don't accept Christ's sacrifice. Do you agree? Why not accept the sacrifice of Jesus for your sins? Why not do it now? It's easy. Simply ask God to forgive you for your sins. Then ask Him to cover your life with the life of Christ. Read John 1:12.

CHAPTER 3

Why God Speaks

Can a Brotha' Get a Word?
"Your word is a lamp to my feet and a light for my path" (Psalm 119:105).

It's not as if this were a minor decision. I had wrestled with it since high school. The arrival of my first year in college only made it worse. As the year progressed I was doing fairly well in school, I had just found the love of my life—although I wasn't so sure at the time, especially when we had "discussions" from time to time—and I was making lots of new friends. Life was good.

But deep in the back of my mind, hidden among the countless axons and dendrites, somewhere betwixt the gray matter, was the nagging desire to know what God wanted me to do in life. What was my career supposed to be? It wasn't too much to ask, was it? All I wanted was a little word on what to study. I was certain that my college wouldn't let me take four years of generals. All God needed to do was sneeze in the direction of my calling, and I was ready to go. No need for a long treatise on the efficacy of one direction or another; just speak the word, Lord. Can a brotha' get a word?

I don't think God took too kindly to my plaintive wails, especially those expressed with ebonic flair. If He did, He sure wasn't telling. *Maybe I'm the problem,* I thought. But then I checked my listening posture, and everything looked right. I went through my waggle like Sergio Garcia standing over a tee shot: praying—check; reading Bible—check; Bible study—half a check; seeking what little wisdom friends had to share—check. Everything seemed to add up, at least in my mind. But somehow I felt as if I were troubling deaf heaven with bootless cries. Heaven was closed for business. Call back later.

39

CAN YOU HEAR ME NOW?

When that all failed, I began to remind the Lord of the time frame.

"Uh, Father, it's now spring, and school is going to be out soon. Now is as good a time as any to let me know whether it's going to be English or theology, biology or accounting. Don't You believe in preplanning?" I asked. I was pretty sure that biology and accounting were off the table, but I threw those in anyway. I was desperate.

Complicating matters was the fact that people close to me kept weighing in on the matter, often when I didn't ask. "Dwain, have you thought about preaching? You should be a minister, bro. You got the stuff!" I neatly tucked that one into file 13, the circular one next to my bed.

"Corporate law, Dwain. You should do that. With your skills you'll be bankin', dude." Now, that one had some legs, especially the bankin' part. I was not averse to a little dinero. But this too sort of fell by the wayside.

After a while I stopped taking advice. I was closed for the summer until further notice. I was going to hear from God and no one else. If He didn't feel it was time to make things clear to me, that was His business. Maybe the thought of my losing my way would scare Him into a little intervention. I didn't know I was playing this game at the time, but I now realize that many of my friends blackmail God in a similar fashion.

They seem to say: "I'm going to kill myself if You don't say something, God. Speak now, or forever hold Your peace." Like the little kid who tells their mother they're going to run away from home, then proceeds to tell her when they're leaving and where they're going, we too hope that God will accede to our demands, change course, and do what we want. Here's a news flash: He's God—as we learned in the first two chapters. He answers when He's ready, and only when He's ready.

God's Word is so powerful that it cannot fail. It simply cannot come back empty (Isaiah 55:11), so don't have a cow just yet. Sometimes His word shines like the floodlights at a Monday night football game, and other times it is barely visible, the faint flicker of a small lamp. At times it's so small that the darkness seems to extinguish it.

While you and I might miss it, misread it, misinterpret it, or misunderstand it, be assured of this: God is still near even when He gets quiet. Perhaps He doesn't want to speak because He's listening to us and He doesn't want to miss a thing.

The answer to my little dilemma didn't come for some time. While I waited, I learned to trust God's timing. I learned to watch for Him, and that's as good as any answer.

Can a brotha' get a word? Yeah, when God is ready.

Why God Speaks

THE 411. . . . .

Do you sometimes long to hear from God on some perplexing subject? You are not alone. In fact, the Bible seems filled with people who at one time or another longed for a word from God. Read Psalm 119:129-136. What role does obedience play in hearing from God?

Dark Planet

"I will not speak with you much longer, for the prince of this world is coming. He has no hold on me" (John 14:30).

Recently scientists have been using satellites deep in space to beam back images of ever more complex pictures of deep, deep space. What they're finding boggles the mind. The pictures depict what appear to be numerous galaxies, such as our Milky Way. The stars defy numbering. Some estimates place the number in the billions. I think it's fairly safe to conclude that we are not alone, that somewhere out there is life. No, not the horrid mutants we see in a *Star Wars* flick. These beings are made in the image of God. They are beautiful.

Also not in dispute is the fact that none of us has ever seen them. There are some folks down here who look like aliens, act like aliens, and (if we're lucky) will one day hop aboard the mother ship and leave the confines of our atmosphere. But in spite of what we might think of our neighbors, they are not from a different world. Ours is the locale in the cosmos where only angels dare tread. We are the quarantine spot in the multiverse. As I heard one preacher remark: "The only being who works down here effectively is God."

Yet we are told in the Bible that there is a rogue in our midst, a being who runs this planet. How he got here is no mystery. The Bible makes it frighteningly clear: "And there was war in heaven. Michael and his angels fought against the dragon, and the dragon and his angels fought back. But he was not strong enough, and they lost their place in heaven. The great dragon was hurled down—that ancient serpent called the devil, or Satan, who leads the whole world astray" (Revelation 12:7-9). How's that for a sci-fi movie?

The Bible spells out that God, Jesus, and the Holy Spirit were in combat with one of Their own, transformed from an angel of light to one of darkness. He lost the battle in heaven, but he's still fighting the war on

41

CAN YOU HEAR ME NOW?

earth. John the revelator continues by showing us who this being is and by warning the inhabitants of earth in Revelation 12:12: "But woe to the earth and the sea, because the devil has gone down to you! He is filled with fury, because he knows that his time is short." Talk about an attitude problem!

Satan is here on earth trying to get back at God for kicking him out of heaven, and you can bet that he's got us in his sights. He is willing to do whatever he can to break our connection with God. Why do you think you can find time to hang with friends, go to the mall, watch a ball game, and work 10-hour days, but not find 10 minutes in the day to worship God? Why is it that everything seems to go great until you decide to get really close to God, to look Him in the eye and make Him Lord of your life? It's not in Satan's best interest to let you have unfettered access to God. So he complicates your life with things, and guess what? We usually let him.

God struggles to get to us, to pry through all the stuff that clutters our life and distorts His voice. He wants to talk to us because, like a man watching a lion stalking caribou in the tall grass, He alone can see the danger. We—the caribou—are oblivious to the danger. God can see Satan's schemes, while we see only the effects of his evil deeds. God sees him when he sets a trap for you. He sees Satan whispering to you when you and your girlfriend go to that spot where nobody can see you. He peers down from a billion miles away as Satan tells you there's nothing wrong with blowing off your parents, because "they had it coming."

God sees, so He tries to help. Sadly, we are not always tuned in to hear His voice. If we are faithful, we too will be able to recognize Satan, even as Jesus did on the night before His betrayal. He was encouraging His disciples as the hour of His crucifixion drew near. Like something out of a horror movie, Jesus could sense that Satan was coming. But He declared victoriously: "He has no hold on me." These words must have steadied the scared disciples.

Jesus wants us to tune in, because only He knows how to defeat Satan.

THE 411. . . . .

What other words of comfort did Jesus speak to His disciples? Read John 14:1-3. Notice, He told His disciples these sayings first. Why didn't He tell them about the devil first?

Why God Speaks

GPS

"Do you not know? Have you not heard? The Lord is the everlasting God, the Creator of the ends of the earth. He will not grow tired or weary, and his understanding no one can fathom" (Isaiah 40:28).

Recently my wife and I took a trip to Atlanta, Georgia. We rented a Ford Taurus from a nearby airport and were delighted to find out that it had a global positioning satellite system. Our car, a 1989 Volvo, has no GPS. It's a really good car—dependable, safe, but not self-directed. It's not connected to the heavens. It's connected to me, and I'm lost most of the time.

The GPS in the Taurus rendered my printed directions unnecessary. All we needed to do was punch in the address of our destination and listen up. The computer system in the car would then download all the directions from the satellite system hovering somewhere in the stratosphere. I must admit this has taken some of the stress out of interstate travel.

However, needless to say, we also had a great time fooling the system. Every time we made an incorrect exit the female voice would begin to get more energetic, less computerized. "Wrong turn," she would say. "Recalculating directions."

It was up to us to follow the directions given. We had to believe that the global positioning system was never wrong. Even when it made a mistake because a road had been changed in name or rerouted, the system recalculated the directions and got us back on our way. As we drove to Atlanta, I couldn't help making the parallels to God. God is all-knowing. He too can see the end from the beginning, and He knows a lot more than directions. When we get off course, God recalculates the directions and puts us back on the path to our destiny. Sounds fairly simple, right?

Well, not exactly. God doesn't seem to speak quite as openly as the computerized woman with the delightful voice does. God is more ethereal. You actually have to do a little work to hear from Him, such as finding out exactly how and where He speaks. But if we are willing to seek the Lord with all our hearts, He promises a reward: "'You will seek me and find me when you seek me with all your heart. I will be found by you,' declares the Lord" (Jeremiah 29:13).

That's right. If we search for God with all we've got, He promises to be found. Heaven's GPS works great, but we need a receiver calibrated to receive God's messages. Once we hook up with heaven, we literally plug into the mind of God, and God's mind is infinite. He knows every challenge we

CAN YOU HEAR ME NOW?

face, every choice we must make, and the outcome of those choices.

At one really difficult period in my life I worked for a boss who just didn't get it. I grew frustrated with the way the office was being run, so I wrote a memo to set some things—and some people—straight. This was no ordinary memo. It would peel the paint off the walls if it got out. Before I sent it to the president of the company and the vice presidents and supervisors, I decided to call my mentor. He usually offers good counsel when I feel like going ballistic. I'm glad I called him.

His counsel was simply: "Burn the memo pronto." I protested mightily, but after much yelling I decided to heed his advice. I'm glad I did. Much later I realized that God used my mentor to help me at a difficult time. Did God have a backup plan if that memo went out? I think so. He would've gone to plan B, if necessary, which in this case would probably have meant finding another job—not exactly God's plan for my life.

One day a few years ago the God positioning system worked for me, and boy, am I happy I made the right choice.

THE 411. . . . .

If you want to find God, read the following scriptures, which provide a blueprint to locating Him: Deuteronomy 4:29, Psalm 105:4, Isaiah 55:6, Hosea 10:12, Luke 11:10. Happy hunting!

I Am the Lord

"And God spoke all these words: 'I am the Lord your God, who brought you out of Egypt, out of the land of slavery'" (Exodus 20:1, 2).

Some experiences you never forget. They follow you around like that tattered pair of shoes you can't quite seem to get rid of. I had one of those experiences when my wife and I decided to spend the Fourth of July holiday with her parents in Los Angeles. We were both looking forward to the break from the stress of work. This was going to be a fun outing.

When we got there, my father-in-law announced that he would be taking me deep-sea fishing off the coast of Catalina Island. Since this was my first time ever doing the deep-sea thing, I jumped at the chance. That morning we rose early. We would need to don the proper attire (dirty clothes), get our gear together, and kiss the girls goodbye. We did so and headed out for the day.

We got on the boat with about 100 men or so. After about an hour

Why God Speaks

into the trip a voice boomed from a loudspeaker.

"All right, gentlemen, you might want to get your poles ready. We've just hit a major school. And they're hungry." The ship's fish detectors had spotted them. Somehow I couldn't get used to the idea of some electronic device finding my fish for me. I guess I had a Captain Ahab complex. I fancied myself the rugged individualist hunting the big one. All such delusions of grandeur were wiped away in one swoop.

The captain's voice made me think of the time Jesus told the distraught disciples to cast their nets overboard after a long night of trolling for fish that never showed. Just as the disciples had, we obeyed.

We threw our lines in, and sure enough, there were large, hungry barracudas down there bent on making a meal of our bait. To my great surprise, it didn't take me long to pull one out. City boy that I am, this was the most fun I'd had in a while. Soon fish were flopping all over the deck of the ship. The day was a total success. Everyone had a great time. Little did I know that my day was just beginning to get interesting.

Everything seemed to be going great until we got back to the shore and prepared to leave the boat. As I reached for my sweater and lunch bag, I noticed that a certain lump in my pocket was missing. My wallet was gone.

By now most of the men were walking off the boat. I was frantic. I walked from one end of the schooner to the other—no wallet. I checked the dining area—no wallet. I looked warily at those still on the boat, scanning for that certain aura of criminality. It was hopeless. Someone must have stolen my wallet, I concluded—either that or it must have fallen out of my pocket while I was fighting one of those barracudas. The former scenario seemed more plausible, since I couldn't bear the thought that I had tossed my life overboard for a barracuda.

On the way home, a sinking feeling filled the pit of my stomach. I was quiet most of the way, hoping that some honest person might find my wallet and return the cash, credit cards, and phone cards. My life was in there. What if the thief decided to use my identity to apply for other credit cards—or worse, buy a car or some other big-ticket item with my name? The thought left me breathless.

I began to pray, asking God to watch over my wallet. Unfortunately, this isn't one of those stories in which the wallet is later found in the middle of a busy street, untouched. I never did get it back.

In the hours following the incident, I worked frantically to close my credit cards and stop all future transactions. Thankfully my identity was preserved, I think.

45

CAN YOU HEAR ME NOW?

As I remember back to that day, I can't help thinking of how important my identity is to my ability to function in society. In an electronic world in which personal data is sold to the highest bidder, one must protect that data at all costs. I imagine that God must feel the same way. No, He is not concerned about His electronic fingerprint being stolen, but He is worried about those who try to assume His identity.

Earth's history is cluttered with the false claims of people who claimed to be God, only to die some ignominious death. Perhaps that is why God so often declared in no uncertain terms that He was the Lord. In Exodus 20 God identifies Himself to a people who had lost all conception of who He was. If you remember the story, God delivered the Israelites from Egyptian bondage *so that they might worship Him in peace.* During the years of captivity the Israelites had forgotten who God was. They had become so infected by idol worship that they had forgotten who God was. So He had to introduce Himself to them again. I am the One who got you out of that Egyptian hellhole. Don't forget Me.

Among the many reasons God chooses to interrupt the goings on here on earth is this: He wants us to know that He is Lord of all.

THE 411 . . . .

In what ways do you forget God? How can you keep God at the helm of your life?

LTs

"Do you have an arm like God's, and can your voice thunder like his?" (Job 40:9).

You know them. You are forced to be around them. They cannot be overlooked no matter how much you bury your face in your salad. They're at your table, and the whole world knows they're with you. You can't hide. The biggest problem with these people is that there's no such thing as a secret. Secrets are told at the level of normal conversation. Anyone who wants to hear can listen in. They are the LTs. You Seinfeld buffs should know the meaning of that acronym, but just in case you missed that episode, LTs are loud talkers.

Contrary to popular belief, these humans with the vocal entrails of a lion are great people to be around—some of the time. They come in handy when the microphones quit working or when the crowd gets too rowdy.

46

Why God Speaks

They're always good for a laugh or two, or some serious embarrassment, which also can be sidesplitting. I know a number of these gifted ones who possess an uncommon ability to violate everyone's personal space from hundreds of yards away. And don't dare give them a cell phone, especially one that's unclear. They'll wake the dead to get their message across.

I remember one especially hilarious moment when a good friend of mine—an LT who shall remain nameless—took me out to dinner. Actually, several of us went together, and I knew that this crew was going to be a raucous bunch. I wasn't mistaken. The joking started when our server came to take our order.

Immediately my friend blurted out something like "Do you guys have any good food in this place?" The server was stunned, and so were we. My friend sensed that the server was shocked, and, feeling a little unsteady, he smiled broadly and burst out laughing. The waiter then understood that this was going to be a fun group, out for a good time. So he played along with us. Before long we had the attention of an entire side of the restaurant. But that was only the beginning. The night climaxed later when the server brought our bill.

My friend, the aforementioned loudmouth, had agreed to pay the bill. He's known for such largeheartedness, and I believe God smiles on him because of it. He's probably the most generous guy I know, but he makes up for it with the embarrassment one usually endures during the meal. On this night he took one look at the bill and yelled at the top of his lungs, "Wwwwwhhhhhaaaattttttt?"

Everyone in the restaurant heard the blood-curdling scream. I guess it's not normal for people to question the items on their bill in such an overt way. This was one of those moments when you wished you could melt into the ground or take a pill that would make you invisible. Everyone in the restaurant was straining to see what was going on. Judging from their faces, I could tell that they were expecting a chair or two to begin flying at any moment.

Our server, who was quite traumatized by this point, looked incredulous. Then he began to smile when he realized my buddy was only joking. He intended to pay the bill, but he just couldn't resist making a scene. We all started laughing, and even the other patrons in the restaurant broke out in laughter. The waiter later told us that we were the most fun group he has ever waited on. It did help that we tipped him rather well.

The Bible tells us of several characters who were LTs. I believe Noah was one. Every day for 120 years he would go out and preach about the

CAN YOU HEAR ME NOW?

coming destruction of the planet. I'm sure his pipes got pretty primed after year 43. I believe David was an LT, though he did make time for quiet reflection with God. Peter, the disciple most likely to die from an overdose of verbiage, had to be an LT. How else does one explain his uncanny ability to speak for the entire core of disciples, not to mention the fact that he was a fisherman? Ever met any quiet fishermen?

Jesus was an LT—at times. Can't you hear His loud, bellowing, commanding voice as He drove the moneychangers from the Temple? Can't you hear Him over the din of the crowd when the woman with the blood problem touched Him? The good thing about Jesus is that, like His Father, He knew when to thunder and when to whisper. The timid felt comfortable in His presence, as did the LTs of His day. He could rap to both groups successfully.

Need a message that is unequivocal? Need a clear, blood-curdling scream from God today? I offer you God, the great LT.

Listen.

THE 411 . . . .

Not buying the "God is an LT" thing? Consider the manner in which His final message to the world will be delivered. Read Revelation 14:6–11. First, notice the content of the angels' messages. That's awesome. Now notice the way in which they deliver that message. What type of voice do they use? What does that tell you about the importance of the message?

That's Enough

"As Paul discoursed on righteousness, self-control and judgment to come, Felix was afraid and said, 'That's enough for now! You may leave. When I find it convenient, I will send for you'" (Acts 24:25).

This was not the best time for the apostle Paul to be holding court about God (Acts 24). The religious leaders were incensed, the Jewish people were ready to tear him limb from limb, and he was now before the governor of Rome. You would think that he'd want to hold off on the Jesus stuff for a while.

Not!

As preachers go, Paul was no Pinto; he was the Rolls-Royce of old-school brick throwers. Everyone who heard him sat spellbound. He was the greatest orator of the early Christian church thanks to the instruction of Gamaliel, a scholar who had taught Paul the art of rhetoric. Paul was a

Why God Speaks

Jew of Jews, a Pharisee of the highest order, and a Roman citizen. He was "Da Man."

It was this latter distinction—being "Da Man"—that seemed to make killing him especially tricky. If he were solely a Jew, devoid of Roman citizenship, the authorities could've hired a hit man, and the deed would have been done. Paul would be pushing up daisies. But, to their utter dismay, Paul had a burgeoning reputation, and he was something of a Houdini.

Rumors flew around Rome about how the Jews had captured him shortly after he began preaching publicly. But then he surfaced in the Roman territories of Perga, Iconium, Lystra, and Derbe. He was on some kind of speaking tour, they heard. He was hardly dead. He went on two more of these missionary jaunts before they really caught him and sent him to the big house—Felix's judgment hall.

The Jewish leaders were infuriated by the teachings of Paul, chiefly because he uplifted Jesus Christ, the same Jesus they had killed just a few decades earlier. So this Paul guy needed killin' real bad. The plot was hatched. They would catch him and turn him over to the Roman authorities. *But what to charge him with?* they wondered.

Some bright bulb in the group came up with a charge. "He's always got large groups of people hollering and saying amen in the streets, right?"

"Yeah," they mused.

"He doesn't hold church in the synagogue the way we do, right?"

"And?" they muttered incredulously.

"Seems to me that that's disturbing the peace. Don't we have laws against that kind of stuff?"

The others nodded their approval, "We do. We have laws for everything!"

"That's it," they concluded. "That's the charge: disturbing the peace."

They petitioned the Roman authorities and got a date for the trial. Everyone expected it to be a spectacle in which Paul would be disgraced and proven the heretic the Jewish leaders thought him to be. Everyone was wrong.

"Most excellent Felix," began Tertullus, the legal eagle hired by the Jewish leaders, "we have found this man to be a troublemaker, stirring up riots among the Jews all over the world. He is a ringleader of the Nazarene [Jesus] sect and even tried to desecrate the temple; so we seized him" (Acts 24:3-6). The air in the great hall was bursting with tension. *How could Paul refute these charges?* the gallery thought.

49

CAN YOU HEAR ME NOW?

Paul's response exposed the weakness of the charges. Just 12 days earlier he had gone to Jerusalem to worship, and no one had accused him of stirring up the people or arguing with the leaders. "They cannot prove to you the charges they are now making against me," Paul noted (verse 13). The crowd was silent as the priests began to squirm.

Then Paul said something that seemed out of place. He had challenged the Jewish leaders to prove their case—and they couldn't. At this point it wasn't necessary for him to declare his beliefs so boldly. However, he seemed compelled by God to do so: "I admit that I worship the God of our fathers as a follower of the Way [Jesus], which they call a sect. I believe everything that agrees with the Law and that is written in the Prophets, and I have the same hope in God as these men, that there will be a resurrection of both the righteous and the wicked. So I strive always to keep my conscience clear before God and man" (verses 14-16).

Paul's words made a big impact on Felix, so much so that he adjourned the meeting and arranged to see Paul privately. Several days later Felix and Drusilla, his wife, went to visit Paul. With no apparent concern for his safety, Paul spoke again about Jesus, about how to be righteous, and about the judgment. Felix was convicted in his heart. He knew that Paul was not only innocent; he was right about who Jesus was.

"That's enough," he shouted. Right then I imagine he instructed the guards to remove Paul. As they hastened, he leaned over to Paul and whispered, "I'll call you back a little later. It's a little inconvenient right now. I've got to run." In that moment his mind became hardened. He had sealed his fate.

Felix thought of his position. If he released Paul he would no longer receive bribes from the Jewish leaders. Secretly he had hoped that Paul would give him a bribe to get out of prison. That's why he came to the prison numerous times over the next two years. He tried to get as much money as he could from the prisoners, since the new governor would take over soon. Each time Felix came, the message was the same: You must accept Jesus Christ to be saved. You must repent. Sadly, Felix refused to change. In fact, as a final favor to the Jewish leaders he left Paul in prison.

This tale of the preacher and the politician teaches many lessons; among them is this: God speaks to us and creates a stage for us to speak for Him. We must take every opportunity to say words that will turn the hearts of others to God. Is it possible that God could have orchestrated Paul's show trial to save Felix? I believe so.

Why God Speaks

Why does God speak to us? He does it so we can share the love of Jesus with others, even if it might mean our peril.

THE 411. . . . .

Take a moment to read the rest of Paul's trial, found in Acts 24, 25, and 26. How did Governor Festus respond to Paul's statements? How did King Agrippa react? Do you notice a trend?

How do you respond when God speaks to you?

The Right Question

"I will do what you have asked. I will give you a wise and discerning heart, so that there will never have been anyone like you, nor will there ever be" (1 Kings 3:12).

Why does God seek to communicate with us? Consider the story of King Solomon at the beginning of his reign, found in 1 Kings 3. This story shouts to us a reality central to understanding why God chooses to answer some prayers and not others.

"Solomon made an alliance with the Pharaoh king of Egypt and married his daughter. He brought her to the City of David until he finished building his palace and the temple of the Lord, and the wall around Jerusalem. The people, however, were still sacrificing at the high places, because a temple had not yet been built for the Name of the Lord. Solomon showed his love for the Lord by walking according to the statutes of his father David, except that he offered sacrifices and burned incense on the high places.

"The king went to Gibeon to offer sacrifices, for that was the most important high place, and Solomon offered a thousand burnt offerings on that altar. At Gibeon the Lord appeared to Solomon during the night in a dream, and God said, 'Ask for whatever you want me to give you.'

"Solomon answered, 'You have shown great kindness to your servant, my father David, because he was faithful to you and righteous and upright in heart. You have continued this great kindness to him and have given him a son to sit on his throne this very day.

"'Now, O Lord my God, you have made your servant king in place of my father David. But I am only a little child and do not know how to carry out my duties. Your servant is here among the people you have chosen, a great people, too numerous to count or number. So give your ser-

51

CAN YOU HEAR ME NOW?

vant a discerning heart to govern your people and to distinguish between right and wrong. For who is able to govern this great people of yours?'

"The Lord was pleased that Solomon had asked for this. So God said to him, 'Since you have asked for this and not for long life or wealth for yourself, nor have asked for the death of your enemies but for discernment in administering justice, I will do what you have asked. I will give you a wise and discerning heart, so that there will never have been anyone like you, nor will there ever be.

"'Moreover, I will give you what you have not asked for—both riches and honor—so that in your lifetime you will have no equal among kings. And if you walk in my ways and obey my statutes and commands as David your father did, I will give you long life.' Then Solomon awoke—and he realized it had been a dream.

"He returned to Jerusalem, stood before the ark of the Lord's covenant and sacrificed burnt offerings and fellowship offerings. Then he gave a feast for all his court" (1 Kings 3:1-15).

THE 411. . . . .

As Bible stories go, this has to be one of the most amazing. Solomon at the beginning of his reign is committing sin—offering sacrifices to foreign gods in the hills. Amid his idolatry God offers him anything he wants. He requests a discerning heart, not for his own benefit, but so that he can be a wise ruler. Wow!

His answer "pleased" God so much that He not only gave him wisdom but riches and the distinction of being the greatest of all earthly kings. If God gave you a similar proposition, what would you ask for? Would it please God?

CHAPTER 4

"Don't You Say That!"

HBO

"For I tell you that unless your righteousness surpasses that of the Pharisees and the teachers of the law, you will certainly not enter the kingdom of heaven" (Matthew 5:20).

This week we'll take a break from examining the unique qualities of God's communication with us and spend some time looking at words that are better left unsaid. I know this is a tangent, but for the rest of this book we'll head off on a few, hopefully making our way back to the main subject from time to time. Anyway, on to the subject of words that are better left unsaid.

Don't you just hate it when people say something about you and then when their verbal indiscretions are proven false they're nowhere to be found?

Think about it for a moment. Have you ever said something about someone or a group of people and wished that you could take it back? Quite often the simplest things said in jest can wound people so completely that healing sometimes takes years.

When I was a kid in junior high school, I remember how tough it was to make it through a day. First of all, I was a recent immigrant to the United States. I came from a country where the language spoken was English, albeit with a few different inflections and sounds.

I stood out like a sore thumb. My clothes were thrift store specials, and I talked funny. I tried my best to sound American. You know, when in Rome do as the Romans do. Just when I thought I was doing pretty well some odd pronunciation would betray me. I just didn't sound right, and I knew it.

Can You Hear Me Now?

And if you didn't sound and look perfectly American, you had problems. Everyone assumed that you had to be Haitian because anyone who wasn't American was Haitian, the catchall group for all American immigrants. The Haitians in junior high, some of the nicest people in the school, had it even worse than I did. They spoke very little English, and they dressed the way I did. Those were two no-no's.

We were constantly asked about what it was like coming over to America on a boat, even though we all flew to America on jets that many of them had only seen on TV. As tough as this was, no putdown was more damning than to be accused of having HBO.

Now you're probably saying, "What's wrong with having the Home Box Office channel?" That's a fair question. There's only one problem, however. The HBO that the kids in my junior high referred to had another meaning. The acronym stood for "Haitian body odor."

It was a putdown that left many students emotionally injured. It was like getting shot. I would see Haitian friends grow quiet and almost sink into the wood floors of our classroom. It was by no means all the kids who engaged in such teasing, but a few ringleaders were enough to get the whole class laughing.

I remember being assaulted once or twice with this jibe. I could endure many things, but this was too much. I internalized the comment so much that I tried to be as clean as possible, wearing every kind of deodorant and cologne I could find, which from time to time might elicit a "Man, you stink" from some other kid.

There just wasn't much the "foreigners" could do to be accepted. Fortunately, after a while the kids would get to know you, and some of them would even stand up for you! I relished such moments, because it meant that I was beginning to be accepted. It also didn't hurt that I did well in school and that some of my classmates needed help, which I was happy to give.

I would help them in order to be accepted. It worked well. However, the more I was accepted, the more I was tempted to engage in the same taunting that had plagued me. I was tempted a few times to shoot the HBO comment at some unsuspecting person, but I always remembered what had happened to me. Occasionally—I'm ashamed to say—I laughed along with some of my friends who were making fun of people.

I do remember making a conscious effort to befriend people who were being put down. I had to wager some of my hard-won cool points to do so, but it was worth it. In this way, I gained many good friends, and I did what was right.

"Don't You Say That!"

Today I remain conscious of inequality and inequity. I look for it. Wherever I see an opportunity to reach out to someone who is looked down upon, I try to take it. I don't always succeed. I don't always do what Jesus would do, but I try.

If I keep trying He will help me, don't you think?

THE 411. . . . .

Read Matthew 25:31-46. Is there a greater challenge in the Bible? In what ways can you be a blessing to someone today?

We may not have food or clothing to give, but when we use our reputations to shield others, when we reach out to those in need without worry about what others will think, we please God.

A Lott of Grief

"The tongue also is a fire, a world of evil among the parts of the body. It corrupts the whole person, sets the whole course of his life on fire, and is itself set on fire by hell" (James 3:6).

"I want to say this about my state—when Strom Thurmond ran for president, we voted for him. We're proud of it. And if the rest of the country had followed our lead, we wouldn't have had all these problems over all these years, either."

Those were the words of former Senate Republican leader Trent Lott, spoken at the 100th birthday celebration for outgoing Senator Strom Thurmond. Seldom in politics are people held accountable for the things they say. From Republicans to Democrats, and everything in between, some politicians make hay with people's biases, with little thought of being held accountable.

No one should be judged on a single statement made in a moment of thoughtlessness. Who hasn't uttered a word or two they wished had never seen the light of day? I know I have. In the case of Senator Lott, this was the final straw that broke the camel's back. Lott represents the state of Mississippi; he of all people should be careful of what he says on issues of race, if for no other reason than the fact that he's from Mississippi, a state with a checkered past on race issues.

To be sure, much has changed in Mississippi since the years when Black people couldn't vote or lived in danger of being lynched. Things have changed for the better. However, there still remains in the South, and

Can You Hear Me Now?

undercover in the North, racist attitudes from a bygone era.

It was to these people that Senator Lott was speaking. His comments were not for general consumption. Politicians know what their core constituents like to hear, and they are sure to say it. That's why during President George W. Bush's first run for the nation's highest office, he spoke at Bob Jones University in South Carolina, even though he knew that the school had outlawed interracial dating and denigrated Catholicism. He needed the Southern vote, and he got it.

In Lott's case, he was referring to the 1948 election in which Senator Strom Thurmond, then a Southern segregationist, ran for president opposing any form of racial integration. In fact, Thurmond's platform sought to overturn, among other things, anti-lynching laws. In this context Lott's statements were explosive, since Thurmond's failed run had long been discredited.

The statement got even more sickening when you parsed the words. What problems was he referring to? The problems of desegregating public schools, the unrest of the 1960s that led to the Civil Rights Act, and the development of affirmative action. Exactly what was he trying to say?

Even more troubling was the fact that Lott has uttered similar sentiments to racist organizations in the past.

As he uttered the words, the room grew somewhat silent. But most of the people there never really got the import of his statements. All the reporters in the room but one missed it. I have a theory that most missed it because they—and we—have become desensitized to racist code words and phrases. We tolerate racial doublespeak.

The same is true of many Black people who tolerate the borderline racist remarks sometimes made by people like Jesse Jackson and Al Sharpton. In either case, people who know better ought to speak out, whether they are Black, White, or green. We should not tolerate racist speech or comments in our presence, even when it comes from people we love and care deeply for.

Lott's comments touched off a firestorm that led to his resignation. He apologized several times in a massive last-ditch effort to save his political career. But it wasn't enough; his own party sacked him, fearing that if he remained majority leader the party would be scrutinized on issues of racial equality and fairness. This was not the kind of attention they wanted.

Lott's words also prove that God's caution concerning the tongue is well founded. Allowed to run amok, the tongue can set the whole person on fire, destroying what took a lifetime to build.

"Don't You Say That!"

So what's the lesson here? Be slow to speak. Measure your words carefully. Better yet, pray before you speak.

THE 411. . . . .

Read James 3:1-12. James is pretty hard on this "little" member of the body. Which bears more responsibility for what comes out of the mouth, the tongue or the mind? Explain.

How can you give God both?

Somethin' to Talk About

"With one heart and mouth you may glorify the God and Father of our Lord Jesus Christ" (Romans 15:6).

You and I were created for God's glory. We were formed to show just how great God is. If we're ever tempted to say something wrong, there's a surefire way to be certain that what we say is right: talk about the goodness of God. You can never go wrong. The psalmist David practiced it quite successfully. God delighted to be in his presence, because David was His friend. David encourages us to praise God at all times.

"I will praise the Lord no matter what happens. I will constantly speak of his glories and grace. I will boast of all his kindness to me. Let all who are discouraged take heart. Let us praise the Lord together, and exalt his name.

"For I cried to him and he answered me! He freed me from all my fears. Others too were radiant at what he did for them. There was no downcast look of rejection! This poor man cried to the Lord—and the Lord heard him and saved him out of all of his troubles. For the Angel of the Lord guards and rescues all who reverence him.

"Oh, put God to the test and see how kind he is! See for yourself the way his mercies shower down on all who trust in him. If you belong to the Lord, reverence him; for everyone who does this has everything he needs. Even strong young lions sometimes go hungry, but those of us who reverence the Lord will never lack any good thing.

"Sons and daughters, come and listen and let me teach you the importance of trusting and fearing the Lord. Do you want a long, good life? Then watch your tongue! Keep your lips from lying. Turn from all known sin and spend your time in doing good. Try to live in peace with everyone; work hard at it.

"For the eyes of the Lord are intently watching all who live good lives,

CAN YOU HEAR ME NOW?

and he gives attention when they cry to him. But the Lord has made up his mind to wipe out even the memory of evil men from the earth. Yes, the Lord hears the good man when he calls to him for help, and saves him out of all his troubles.

"The Lord is close to those whose hearts are breaking; he rescues those who are humbly sorry for their sins. The good man does not escape all troubles—he has them too. But the Lord helps him in each and every one. God even protects him from accidents.

"Calamity will surely overtake the wicked; heavy penalties are meted out to those who hate the good. But as for those who serve the Lord, he will redeem them; everyone who takes refuge in him will be freely pardoned" (Psalm 34, TLB).

Now, that's something to talk about. God is not good; He's great!

THE 411. . . . .

In the October 16, 1883, issue of the *Review and Herald,* author Ellen G. White commented on verses 12-15 of Psalm 34. Here's what she said: "The assurance of God's approval will promote physical health. It fortifies the soul against doubt, perplexity, and excessive grief, that so often sap the vital forces and induce nervous diseases of a most debilitating and distressing character. . . . We make very hard work for ourselves in this world when we take such a course that the Lord is against us."

Hard Times

"Six days you shall labor, but on the seventh day you shall rest; even during the plowing season and harvest you must rest" (Exodus 34:21).

Her words caught me by surprise. She was an Israeli woman, a Jew. She described herself as a Sabbath believer, yet her statement seemed at odds with this pronouncement. Here's what happened.

I was driving home from work one day when a news segment on National Public Radio caught my attention. Actually it was the word *Sabbath* that made me perk up. As a Sabbath believer in a society in which the majority of people worship on Sunday, one rarely hears Sabbath mentioned in the media. What's more, the entire story addressed the Sabbath as it is kept and practiced in Israel.

I think it's fair to say that Jews are somewhat of an authority on the Sabbath. While many believe that the Sabbath originated with them,

"Don't You Say That!"

Genesis 1 and 2 make it clear that God created the Sabbath at the beginning of earth's history. It was a gift to all people, long before God chose Abraham's descendants to be His special representatives to the world.

When God gave the Ten Commandments to Moses, He shared them with the Jews. The fourth commandment was a special reminder of God's ownership of all and a memorial of His creation. The Sabbath was to be set aside from every other day of the week. It was holy.

Therefore, the Jews were warned: "Do not light a fire in any of your dwellings on the Sabbath day" (Exodus 35:3). When Nehemiah rebuilt the walls of Jerusalem, during the dedication ceremony he gave this admonition: "When the neighboring peoples bring merchandise or grain to sell on the Sabbath, we will not buy from them on the Sabbath or on any holy day" (Nehemiah 10:31).

Even today the Sabbath remains a central institution in Jewish life. It punctuates each week. Most of the shops and malls in Israel are closed on Saturday, the Sabbath. Most of the Jews go to the synagogue to worship God.

With this background in mind, I was surprised to hear the Jewish woman say, "It's OK to pray to God, but we have to do something to help ourselves. We have to open our store on the Sabbath. Things are really bad right now."

For a moment I could not help sympathizing with her. The reality is that the threat of suicide bombings has paralyzed Israeli society, especially when it comes to shopping. During the workweek few people venture out to the malls. Hence, Sabbath is quickly becoming the shopping day of choice.

The Jewish business owner reported that business has been doubling each Sabbath that she opens her clothing store in the mall. Her posture seems to be: hard times call for desperate measures. When times get tough, honoring God takes a back seat.

Even as she uttered the words, she pleaded for understanding from other business owners who refused to open their stores. One young man, owner of a clothing store, spoke of the importance of the Sabbath in his life. "I've kept the Sabbath all my life. It's all I know. I won't change now."

I don't want to be too hard on the businesswoman who decided to open on the Sabbath. Difficult choices face every person, and we don't always make the right choice. All of us are at different stages of growth. However, I couldn't help wondering at the irony of the situation. When we obey God's Word and keep the Sabbath holy, we say in effect, "God, I believe in You. You made this world. You made me, and I know that no matter what happens on earth, You will take care of me."

Can You Hear Me Now?

I was struck by her words because she was giving up the very thing that would help her through the financial crisis she faced. It made me wonder whether I would obey God in times of crisis.

I hope I will. Will you?

THE 411. . . . .
Read Exodus 20:8-11 and Isaiah 58:13 and 14. Why is God so serious about the Sabbath? Ask God to help you not only to keep His Sabbath holy but also to stand up for Him no matter what you face.

Shut Up!

"Will your long-winded speeches never end? What ails you that you keep on arguing?" (Job 16:3).

Recently I was sharing some of my frustrations with a friend. He was pretty understanding, since we both had experienced similar trials and tribulations.

You probably won't be able to appreciate this episode fully unless you live in a major city. I trust that it never happens to you.

I had the unfortunate privilege of having to retrieve my car after the city's abandoned vehicles division had towed it. It was not one of my finer moments as a Christian, I can assure you.

I drove from Hagerstown, Maryland—a three-hour tour—to Philadelphia with the mistaken idea that I would be able to get my car out of the salvage yard to which it had been towed.

I got home about 2:00 p.m., plenty of time to get my vehicle back. Earlier I had gotten my car insured and registered with new license plates to spare. I was ready for any eventuality, I thought.

The last hitch was getting a ride to the salvage yard. My neighbor, Mr. Brown, a wonderful older gentleman, solved that problem when he offered to take me. Everything was falling into place, I thought.

We drove to the site where the car was, getting there about 4:00 p.m., only to find that there was no sign signaling that this was indeed Lou's Salvage Yard. We decided to venture inside anyway.

The building was cold and dingy. A dog well past its prime lay motionless behind the counter. Greasy men would surface from time to time from the back of the building, helping customers find used parts. This was a hellhole from which I hoped to escape with all deliberate speed.

"Don't You Say That!"

"Is this Lou's Salvage?" I asked. A girl who looked to be about 18 to 20 years old came to the counter. Another guy sat over to the left of her, but it was obvious that she was running this show.

"Yes, this is Lou's. How may I help you?"

I explained to her that my car had been towed, and pulled out my information. I had called ahead a day earlier and found out from the manager what I needed to bring in order to get my car released.

"Just bring your driver's license, registration, and proof of insurance, pay the towing fee, and the car is yours." I was elated. That sounded easy enough. No problem.

I showed all my information to the young woman, and she made photocopies of everything. I paid her and asked her to show me to my car. That's when I entered the twilight zone.

"I'm sorry, but I cannot release your car to you." At first I wasn't sure what she said, so I just looked blankly at her. Perhaps this was their way of relieving the tension of anxious people who came in search of their cars. It wasn't funny, and I wasn't laughing.

"What do you mean?" I inquired.

"Sir, your car has not been inspected. You cannot drive your car off this lot. You must have it towed off the property; then you can drive it from there."

By this time Mr. Brown, my neighbor, was standing outside his car looking in. He could see from my expression that something was wrong.

"No, you don't understand," I retorted. "I called here and asked specifically what I needed to bring to retrieve my car. I brought those items. What are you talking about?" My voice began to rise.

"I cannot release the car to you, sir. It has not been inspected, and the law prohibits me from releasing the car." By now her constant refrain was getting more and more irritating.

I was irate, but I had to be careful. Recently Kemba and I have been making an effort to share Jesus Christ with our neighbors. This was not the time to lose my mind, but this was a battle I was quickly losing.

"But the law says clearly that after registering the vehicle I have 10 days to get it inspected. I'm not even registering my vehicle in Pennsylvania. Pennsylvania law does not matter here. Even if I was registering my vehicle in Pennsylvania, by law I still have five days to get it inspected. I can't do that if I cannot drive it off the lot."

I might as well have been yelling at a brick. She was unmoved by my rather persuasive argument. I would have to have my car towed off the lot,

61

CAN YOU HEAR ME NOW?

and then I could drive it. What's more, the time was approaching 5:00 p.m., and she made it clear that they would not be able to stay open after 5:00 to wait for a tow truck to come.

I felt as if I had just entered Bizarro World. This was a planet I knew not.

Mr. Brown came in and pleaded my case, but to no avail. She was resigned to her conclusion.

In my mind I searched for just the right mix of cursewords to shower on her. I knew them well. I'd even tried some of them out as a teenager, but something stopped me. Something said, "Don't you say that. Don't you dare utter those words." I knew it was God's Holy Spirit trying to slow the train of my anger.

I felt like telling her to shut up, then swiftly hopping over the counter. I've vowed to never hit a woman, but on that afternoon my vow was severely tested.

However, I simply decided to leave. On the way home I tried to cool my anger. Mr. Brown encouraged me not to get upset. With age comes a certain serenity that I wish I had.

The next morning I prepared to go with my wife to get the car. We prayed about the situation, and she decided to call ahead. I was in no mood to talk to anyone at Lou's Salvage Yard. In my heart I had already murdered everyone at Lou's. I needed God's forgiveness.

Kemba wasn't on the phone for one minute before the person at the other end began apologizing. Scott, one of the managers there, had heard about the incident and was very sorry about what had happened to us.

"She should have let you have your car," he said. "She was mistaken. There's no way that we can keep your car after you've showed proof of registration and insurance. I'm sorry for the inconvenience." Later that morning we went and retrieved the car without a hitch.

There are anxious times in life when we desperately need to know that God is with us, taking care of everything. During my experience at the salvage yard I forgot that singular fact. I decided to depend on myself. I thought that I had worked everything out and that things would happen without a hitch. I was wrong.

In the final analysis, nothing on earth works out as planned if God is not in control, guiding everything. He is the great equalizer, the grease that smoothes the rough edges of life.

THE 411. . . . .

Read Job 16. In this chapter Job grows weary of his "friends'" finger-

"Don't You Say That!"

pointing. At a time when he needed encouragement, they were "dogging" him, accusing him of crimes against God.

Did Job respond to his friends in anger? How do you respond when you get worked up?

Too Much Information

"How do you know that Saul and his son Jonathan are dead?" (2 Samuel 1:5).

Who hasn't done it? A carefully placed word or two to the right person can change one's entire existence. So countless persons each day risk it all to get a leg up on a competitor or coworker, earnestly desiring to win the confidence of some influential person. However, things don't always work out as planned.

Consider the following story found in 2 Samuel 1. It makes for fascinating reading.

"After the death of Saul, David returned from defeating the Amalekites and stayed in Ziklag two days. On the third day a man arrived from Saul's camp, with his clothes torn and with dust on his head. When he came to David, he fell to the ground to pay him honor.

" 'Where have you come from?' David asked him.

"He answered, 'I have escaped from the Israelite camp.'

" 'What happened?' David asked. 'Tell me.'

"He said, 'The men fled from the battle. Many of them fell and died. And Saul and his son Jonathan are dead.'

"Then David said to the young man who brought him the report, 'How do you know that Saul and his son Jonathan are dead?'

" 'I happened to be on Mount Gilboa,' the young man said, 'and there was Saul, leaning on his spear, with the chariots and riders almost upon him. When he turned around and saw me, he called out to me, and I said, "What can I do?"

" 'He asked me, "Who are you?"

" ' "An Amalekite," I answered.

" 'Then he said to me, "Stand over me and kill me! I am in the throes of death, but I'm still alive."

" 'So I stood over him and killed him, because I knew that after he had fallen he could not survive. And I took the crown that was on his head and the band on his hand and have brought them here to my lord.'

"Then David and all the men with him took hold of their clothes and

63

CAN YOU HEAR ME NOW?

tore them. They mourned and wept and fasted till evening for Saul and his son Jonathan, and for the army of the Lord and the house of Israel, because they had fallen by the sword.

"David said to the young man who brought him the report, 'Where are you from?'

"'I am the son of an alien, an Amalekite,' he answered.

"David asked him, 'Why were you not afraid to lift your hand to destroy the Lord's anointed?'

"Then David called one of his men and said, 'Go, strike him down!' So he struck him down, and he died. For David had said to him. 'Your blood be on your own head. Your own mouth testified against you when you said, "I killed the Lord's anointed"'" (verses 1-15).

The brave young Amalekite had managed to get away from the Israelites. He was no doubt apprehended in close proximity to Saul's body. As an enemy of Israel he would no doubt die for his involvement in the death of Saul.

After his daring escape, however, he reasoned that the one person who would appreciate the news of Saul and Jonathan's death was David. After all, he surmised, Saul was David's adversary. Surely the man who delivered Saul's head would occupy a great place in David's kingdom, alien or no alien.

He reasoned wrong.

Furthermore, he added one juicy tidbit, which got him executed. He told of how he killed Saul after Saul asked him to. This should have been a mitigating factor, but David was incredulous. "How could you kill God's anointed one?" he asked. "I too had several opportunities to kill him, but I restrained myself. Why did you do it?"

I'm certain the young lad was surprised by the reaction he received. David and his men tore their garments and wept at the death of Saul and Jonathan. Then David gave the order to kill the young Amalekite.

There's so much we can learn from this tale. For one, it shows that true love for God and His people should not change based on whether they obey God or not. David loved Saul in spite of his behavior. That said, we can also take away a lesson on the importance of knowing one's audience and measuring one's speech. Playing the influence game is a dangerous endeavor. It's better to have God exalt you in His time.

THE 411. . . . .

Did David respect Saul, or his position as king of Israel? What does this tell you about how we should respect those chosen by God to lead? Did David's respect for Saul mean that he approved of Saul's behavior?

"Don't You Say That!"

The Fall of Jericho

"'Do not shout; do not even talk,' Joshua commanded" (Joshua 6:10, NLT).

The fall of Jericho is a story you probably know very well. It's the amazing conquest of a rival nation that occurs without so much as a drawn sword.

The Israelites were directed by God to march around the city each day in total silence. How's that for a battle strategy? Imagine how the people in Jericho felt. There are moments when total silence is louder than a million cannons.

The fear that the citizens of Jericho felt was palpable. Something was about to happen. We pick up the story on the first day.

"Now the gates of Jericho were tightly shut because the people were afraid of the Israelites. No one was allowed to go in or out. But the Lord said to Joshua, 'I have given you Jericho, its king, and all its mighty warriors. Your entire army is to march around the city once a day for six days. Seven priests will walk ahead of the Ark, each carrying a ram's horn.'

"'On the seventh day you are to march around the city seven times, with the priests blowing the horns. When you hear the priests give one long blast on the horns, have all the people give a mighty shout. Then the walls of the city will collapse, and the people can charge straight into the city.'

"So Joshua called together the priests and said, 'Take up the Ark of the Covenant, and assign seven priests to walk in front of it, each carrying a ram's horn.' Then he gave orders to the people: 'March around the city, and the armed men will lead the way in front of the Ark of the Lord.'

"After Joshua spoke to the people, the seven priests with the rams' horns started marching in the presence of the Lord, blowing the horns as they marched. And the priests carrying the Ark of the Lord's covenant followed behind them. Armed guards marched both in front of the priests and behind the Ark, with the priests continually blowing the horns.

"'Do not shout; do not even talk,' Joshua commanded. 'Not a single word from any of you until I tell you to shout. Then shout!' So the Ark of the Lord was carried around the city once that day, and then everyone returned to spend the night in the camp" (Joshua 6:1-11, NLT).

"On the seventh day the Israelites got up at dawn and marched around the city as they had done before. But this time they went around the city seven times. The seventh time around, as the priests sounded the long blast on their horns, Joshua commanded the people, 'Shout! For the Lord has given you the city!'" (verses 15, 16, NLT).

CYHMN-3

CAN YOU HEAR ME NOW?

THE 411. . . . .

The walls of Jerusalem were so massive and thought to be so impregnable that the Jebusites taunted David and his commander, Joab, saying: "You will not get in here; even the blind and the lame can ward you off" (2 Samuel 5:6). Turns out they were right. It took an act of God.

CHAPTER 5

How God Speaks

Loud and Clear

"His feet were like bronze glowing in a furnace, and his voice was like the sound of rushing waters" (Revelation 1:15).

As we learned from the fall of Adam and Eve in Genesis 3, sin can change the way we hear and see God. Sometimes God struggles to get through the hip-hop of life, hoping that we will turn down the volume of sin low enough for His Holy Spirit to be heard. However, every now and then God raises His voice—and, man, it's effective, but it sure ain't pretty. Let me explain.

It was Thursday, and I was preparing to leave work to go home. My commute is slightly longer than most, about two and a half hours longer. It's something I've been doing for several months now since my move from Hagerstown, Maryland, to Philadelphia, Pennsylvania.

No, I don't commute back and forth every day. Usually I drive to Hagerstown on Monday and return to Philadelphia on Thursday. It's not the greatest schedule, but life doesn't always deal you a great hand. Sometimes you've got to play the hand you're dealt.

As I prepared to leave, I ran into one of my coworkers. Needless to say, I wasn't thrilled. On Thursdays I'm usually in a rush to leave work, so any interruptions that alter my flight plan are usually met with cold stares and glares. At home waiting for me is a hottie—that's wife to you—whom I haven't seen in four days. You get my drift?

Anyway, we began talking about my trek to Philly.

"So, you really do this every week?" she asked.

67

Can You Hear Me Now?

"Yes, I do," I offered shortly.

"It must take you at least, what, two to three hours to get home, right?"

"Yeah, about that." By now I was ready to escape, but I didn't want to be rude. Walking off in midrant would probably not be a good idea, though the thought was tempting. And most of my coworkers think I'm a nice guy—no need to burst the bubble of naïveté that has served me so well. There'll be plenty of time to do that later.

That's when she hit me right between the eyes. She didn't physically smash my grille, but she might as well have.

"You know, that's a great time to really do some thinking," she noted. "Did you know that Ellen White says that if we took one hour a day to contemplate the life of Christ it would change our lives? That would be a great time to think about Jesus."

Her words hung in the air thickly, almost visible. She had hit a nerve in my spiritual life. There's nothing quite like a carefully timed E. G. White quote to challenge your Christianity.

Immediately my thoughts started racing. *But what about my favorite news stations; what about my music tapes? (I don't have a CD player in my car.) Who could spend two to three hours thinking about Jesus? There ain't that much Jesus in the Bible, right?*

I finally mustered up some words. "You know, that's a great idea. I should try that." With that I said goodbye and left.

As I started for home, the thought continued to nag me. *It can't hurt. Turn the radio off and try it. What do you have to lose but some down time?*

Then it was as if I heard God say, "I'm ready to talk. Spend some time with Me, and you will be blessed."

I obeyed. I turned the radio off and focused on a Scripture passage in Matthew. Jesus, on His way into Jerusalem, sees a fig tree and approaches it to pick something to eat. To His utter horror, the tree was green, beautiful, and barren. No figs in sight. The tree so upset its Maker that Jesus cursed it and pronounced, "May you never bear fruit again!" (Matthew 21:18).

I started to think about the power Jesus had at His disposal. How was it possible that immediately after His curse the tree began to wither? It's as though He withdrew its life source, as though He cut Himself off from it, since He is life (John 14:6). Apart from Him, nothing can live.

The voice that beckoned me to silent meditation grew louder as I meditated on Jesus. I could hear God's voice loudly in my mind, so much so that it was deafening. Again the voice said, *You must totally surrender your life to Me if you want the power that Jesus had.*

How God Speaks

It continued: *The tree was cursed because it soaked up God's sunlight, rain, and nutrients, yet bore no fruit. That tree represents those who have everything that pertains to salvation (the Bible, the Spirit of Prophecy, the life of Christ), yet they bear no fruit. If you give Me a chance, I'll give you power to change your life and power to change the world. I love you, son. Make time for Me! Put Me first!*

Before long I looked at my watch, only to discover that I had spent one hour and 45 minutes in prayerful meditation on the life and ministry of Jesus. The time seemed to fly like the wind.

The voice of God was louder and clearer than anything I'd ever heard before. He was booming His message into my ear. The sound was not some externally audible voice; it was an internal primal scream that made my mind feel alive, elevated, high. For those precious moments the temptations that I struggle with seemed to lose their grasp. For an instant I was with God in His presence. There I found fullness of joy and pleasures forevermore (Psalm 16:11).

THE 411. . . . .

How does God speak to you? Do you take time to listen? Do you set aside undivided, uninterrupted time to hear Him? Today set aside 10, 20, or 30 minutes—whatever sounds doable for you—and ask God to meet with you. Read a portion of Scripture, and then listen to God.

Animal Speak

"But ask the animals, and they will teach you, or the birds of the air, and they will tell you" (Job 12:7).

Some people act like animals, and some animals act the way people should. That's the only explanation for some of the "bonehead" things we "higher creations" do from time to time.

"Too harsh a criticism," you say? Then how are we to explain the phenomenon of Howard Stern, New York's resident ingrate and all-around pervert? How do we account for the Ariel Sharons and the Yasir Arafats? the Jeffrey Dahmers and Ted Bundys? How do we evaluate the morality of nations who have enough food to feed every hungry child on the planet, yet pay farmers to destroy or underproduce crops?

How do we explain the growing gap between rich and poor nations? Are all the poor people in the world lazy blokes who don't want to work,

CAN YOU HEAR ME NOW?

or are they the unwitting pawns of despots, multinational corporations, and "civilized" developed nations?

There really is no explanation for the strangeness of human behavior. We can only conclude that amid the din and turmoil of living in this lost world we become stripped of our humanity, our sense of right and wrong, our decency. What we have on Planet Earth today is sin run amok, and anyone who wants to stay here forever is "a few fries short of a happy meal."

But there's good news, for where "sin increased, grace increased all the more," says the apostle Paul (Romans 5:20).

Juxtaposed against the crazy antics of humans, however, is the consistency of obedience shown by virtually all animals. Imagine standing next to Noah on the day when God gave the command to let the animals into the ark.

Picture the scene. An old man known to be a bit of a kook comes out each day and preaches a terrible message of imminent destruction by rain and flood, elements never seen or experienced before on earth. Surely we can sympathize with the skeptical onlookers. Not only does he preach each day, but he does so for 120 years. Now, that's a long sermon. Remember that the next time your pastor preaches for an hour.

Noah's verbal barrage was amazing in itself, but what happened next really strained credulity.

"On that very day Noah and his sons, Shem, Ham and Japheth, together with his wife and the wives of the three sons, entered the ark. They had with them every wild animal according to its kind, all livestock according to their kinds, every creature that moves along the ground according to its kind and every bird according to its kind, everything with wings. Pairs of all creatures that have the breath of life in them came to Noah and entered the ark.

"The animals going in were male and female of every living thing, as God had commanded Noah. Then the Lord shut him in" (Genesis 7:13-16).

That's one of the most mind-altering passages in God's Word. If the people on the earth at the time didn't like Noah's old school rap, his tired 'gators, played-out bell-bottoms, and half-bald 'fro, they had one other unmistakable, unimpeachable, undeniable proof of what was to come. They had the testimony of the animals.

Sadly, the same myopia afflicts many of us today. We fail to examine God's creation, to listen for its hidden refrain. Behind the lion's roar, the owl's piercing gaze, the hyena's smile, the elephant's longevity, the turtle's ironclad shell, is God.

Two by two the animals marched into the ark, lambs and tigers, bears

70

How God Speaks

and sheep, bugs and giraffes—all testifying in their own way about the existence of God, all communicating an important message to their intelligent earthly masters, who seemed to act only on instinct.

THE 411. . . . .

When Job's friends laughed at tragic misfortune and concluded that he had done something to incur God's wrath, Job's response is profound. Read Job 12 to see what I mean.

Notice what he says about the animals (verses 7-9). Job intimates that if the animals could speak, they would testify that he had done nothing wrong and that God had allowed these things to befall His servant.

Strange Messenger

"There is still one man through whom we can inquire of the Lord, but I hate him because he never prophesies anything good about me, but always bad" (1 Kings 22:8).

Today I got a call from a great friend. His name is Tim. He is a man of God, a fan of all Philadelphia sports, and a criminal defense attorney. If I were ever to face the penalty of jail, or worse, execution, I'd first talk to God. But right after talking with God, I would get on the horn to Tim. He is quite good at his craft.

Tim would be the first to admit that he has defended people who were indeed guilty of the crimes for which they were prosecuted. He has also seen his share of innocent people sacrificed on the altar of political expediency and prosecutorial misconduct, to say nothing of dishonest police officers.

On this day, however, Tim is calling to tell me the latest developments in the case of a troubled young man accused of a string of very serious robberies. Tim felt he had a good chance of getting several charges dropped or dismissed.

Two victims had failed to pick Tim's client out of a police lineup, and a few other witnesses in the case had left the country. Several charges remained, but he could argue police coercion on some of them, and on others he could make a case that the overzealous prosecutors were rushing to judgment.

On this day he called me to announce that the prosecutors had walked into court that morning and had dropped eight of the robbery charges against his client. It was a vindication of Tim's strategy and the general weakness of the state's case. One very serious charge remained, however,

CAN YOU HEAR ME NOW?

and Tim knew his client stood a good chance of being convicted on that charge, but he was hopeful.

The accused was in jail during the court proceedings in which the charges were dropped. He was totally unaware. His parents were ecstatic at this turn of events. They had been through another lawyer—who urged their son to plead guilty to all the charges—before they asked Tim to represent their son. They were absolutely flabbergasted when they saw the outcome. They were happy. Alas, their boy had another chance to make his life right. They knew he was no saint, and they admitted it.

Overjoyed, Tim hurried to the prison where his client was being held to deliver the good news. What he found was a calm, well-dressed, serene young man. The hollow nonchalance that once characterized him was gone.

"John," Tim began excitedly, "I've got some good news for you. The DA dropped eight of the charges against you."

John hardly batted an eyebrow. "I knew they would," he responded calmly. "I prayed about it. It's all in God's hands. I'm not worried about anything."

The client, who seemed to lack any semblance of spiritual rectitude, seemed transformed. His words caught Tim by surprise and left him somewhat speechless.

As we talked about the young client's amazing statement, Tim noted, "I saw God today."

The client's words resonated with both Tim and me because we have talked often about the tough times in life when we have dreaded getting out of bed to face the day. Here was someone facing several decades of jail-time acting as though nothing in the world could ruin his day.

He was an odd messenger for such a profound message. Surely this is what you'd expect from a preacher or from your mother. Not exactly the kind of thing people in prison say.

In the various seasons of life we must always remember that God speaks through people—of all stripes, colors, nationalities, and creeds. He is an equal opportunity user. Any willing person can become a conduit of God's divine Word.

Would you accept God's message if it came from some unexpected source, someone you had written off?

THE 411. . . . .
Read the story of Micaiah the prophet, found in 1 Kings 22:1-39.

How God Speaks

Why did Ahab hate Micaiah so much? If we listen only to the people we like, who tell us what we want to hear, what might happen to us?

Talk to Me!

"Through Jesus, therefore, let us continually offer to God a sacrifice of praise— the fruit of lips that confess his name" (Hebrews 11:15).

I love my wife's voice. It's soft, easy like a trickling stream, deliberately calm, and serene. It gently caresses my inner ear with the subtlety of a water lily in a pond. She speaks peace to me.

You should hear her say, "Hi. How are you?" or the special "Hi, Dwain" that greets me when I return home at the end of a long week. There are few things more precious to me than those simple words accompanied by her smile. (On second thought, don't even talk to her. Smile.)

I won't even bother to mention the "I love you"s she is prone to drop at just the right time. If she makes the mistake of letting one of those fly, she knows I'm putty in her hands. She can get anything she wants. "Just talk to me," I shout to her. "I'm yours!"

It's not just the sweet somethings that sets Kemba apart from every other woman on the planet; it's the life she lives that adds meaning to her words.

Every "Hi, Dwain" is backed by countless hours spent working out our finances. Yes, my wife is the resident financial genius in our home. You probably don't want me near anything of monetary value.

Every "I love you" is supported by numerous prayers and Bible study, warm hugs, soft kisses, and priceless gifts. Kemba's words are but mere tokens of the life she lives.

I guess what my wife does for me can be described only as ministry, that odd thing God calls us to do for each other. It's no easy task, however. My wife will be the first to tell you that there's no one on earth who could hurt her the way I can. Who else could be so cold and dismissive, distant and selfish? I'm the one Homo sapien who knows the code.

She hurts from time to time, because she has risked her heart to love me deeply. If you hope never to hurt, there's a sure way to achieve that end. Never love. But something tells me you're going to give love a shot.

If you ever decide to do so, ask God to send you someone who will excite you spiritually. Unfortunately, our declining culture encourages relationships built on money, sex, fun, and little else. There's no considera-

CAN YOU HEAR ME NOW?

tion of spiritual compatibility, no thought of one's God quotient.

Having been on this side of marriage, I cannot help wondering, What will Joe Sex-Starved say to Jane Sex-Ready when one of them breaks the marital vow? Who will be left to pick up the pieces if God's not in the mix?

What will they say to each other when one of them is fired from a dream job, or miscarries a child, or contracts some terminal disease?

What will they tell each other when the world really begins to come apart at its seams, when children betray their parents and vice versa? Who will tell them that God is near when sudden destruction comes?

When we don't allow God to select our lover, we shortchange ourselves and them, because God often prepares a special pick-me-up and hand-delivers it to us through them.

I can't help thanking God for a woman who daily offers to Him, and her husband, the "sacrifice of praise—the fruit of lips that confess his name."

THE 411. . . . .

Do you have some special person in your heart? Have you committed them to God? Have you asked God to give you someone through whom He can minister to you?

Liar!

"Whenever I speak, I cry out proclaiming violence and destruction. So the word of the Lord has brought me insult and reproach all day long" (Jeremiah 20:8).

Nobody likes a liar—except maybe other liars adept at spinning a tantalizing yarn. One who tells lies, whether they be verbal fabrications, furtive glances, or dismissive looks, seems to suck a little goodness out of the world with each prevarication.

Surely God can't be thought of as one who accepts such behavior. The Bible makes it clear that if truth serum were ever needed to determine who was telling the truth—God or us—"let God be true, and every man a liar" (Romans 3:4). I can hear the women applauding that statement. In fact, I know some women who think all men are truth-challenged and resemble a certain animal that shall remain nameless.

So you might imagine that God would take offense to someone calling Him by the L word. "O Lord, you deceived me, and I was deceived" (Jeremiah 20:7). OK, OK. So Jeremiah didn't use the L word, but deceiver is close enough. Just ask Satan, called a deceiver and the father of lies by

How God Speaks

none other than the Son of God. To associate God with the archfiend of the universe sort of gets heaven's attention.

As if that's not enough to warrant a few laser-guided lightning bolts, Jeremiah presses his luck further, saying, "You overpowered me and prevailed."

Let me see if I have this right. Jeremiah has just called God a liar. Sounds crazy, right? But he goes on to say that God is a thug, a gangsta, and a con man who overpowers him and forces him to do a painful deed.

Jerry doesn't stop there, however. *If you're feeling suicidal, why not go all the way and get yourself killed?* he seems to conclude. "I am ridiculed all day long; everyone mocks me," he yells at God as the anguish he feels creases his furrowed brow.

But before we tar and feather Jeremiah, we must remember that he was most likely a teenager when he was given an impossible task. "Before I formed you in the womb I knew you," God told him at the beginning of his ministry. "Before you were born I set you apart; I appointed you as a prophet to the nations" (Jeremiah 1:5). Jeremiah must have wondered, *Couldn't You wait a few more years?*

God had given young Jerry a message to give to the people of Judah, only this message would not help him win friends and influence people. He would be hated, reviled, and persecuted. But, as he so eloquently noted, God deceived him, or so he thought.

Needless to say, God didn't lie to young Jerry. When young Jeremiah expressed fear and apprehension at his new calling, God reassured him. "Do not be afraid of them, for I am with you and will rescue you" (verse 8).

This was Jeremiah's moment to vent, and God was not going to interrupt him. That's one of the truly great qualities of God. He is confident and self-assured enough to tolerate the ranting and raving of peons He could squash with a simple thought.

Truth is, Jerry was a little banged up. His face bore the scars of numerous slaps. Several fresh ridges were cut into his back as a result of whippings. And to add further insult, he was placed in the stocks "at the Upper Gate of Benjamin at the Lord's temple" (Jeremiah 20:2). Pashhur, chief officer of the Temple and resident enforcer in the priestly ranks, had ordered the harsh treatment after he heard Jeremiah prophesying about what God told him to say.

It was a no-win situation for God. Jerry was hurt, and God knew it was the pain talking. He knew that Jerry's heart would heal and that he would go back to his mission. God was right, for Jeremiah continued to

CAN YOU HEAR ME NOW?

plead with the people of Judah to stave off the captivity of the Babylonians.

This episode tells us much about how God speaks. For one, God's silence in times of deep despair is a form of speech. Perhaps He is saying, "I'm listening. It's good to finally have your undivided attention, even if you are calling Me names."

Maybe He's communicating this message: "Trust My word when I seem far away." That's little comfort to a hurting heart, but these are the precious instances when character is forged, spiritual muscles developed, and discipline taught.

When you feel bamboozled, hoodwinked, cajoled by God, that's when He is nearest. So rant a bit, but come back home.

THE 411. . . . .

My friend Ellen G. White writes, "The trials of life are God's workmen, to remove the impurities and roughness from our character. Their hewing, squaring, and chiseling, their burnishing and polishing, is a painful process. . . . But the stone is brought forth prepared to fill its place in the heavenly temple" (*Thoughts From the Mount of Blessing,* p. 10).

Sin Changes Things

"Then the man and his wife heard the sound of the Lord God as he walked in the garden in the cool of the day, and they hid from the Lord God among the trees of the garden" (Genesis 1:8).

Friday the 13th. Halloween. A Nightmare on Elm Street. Hellraiser. If you recognize any of those titles, chances are you've made the mistake of watching one of these movies and endured the nightmares that follow. Perhaps, you're one of those "special" people who can sit through a super-size serving of Freddy Krueger, Jason, and Pumpkinhead. However, I am not, and while I'm thinking about it, let me drop this subtle nugget of wisdom on you: STOP WHILE YOU CAN. YOU ARE FRYING YOUR BRAIN—not to mention your relationship with God.

I remember watching a Friday 13th flick several years ago—yes, I'm getting old. Something about it lured me in and piqued my interest. The plot was like all the other Jason plots. Cute, unsuspecting teenagers escape to some faraway cabin by a lonely, dreary lake.

They are not there to take in the joys of nature. The outing is basically a thinly veiled grope session. They're there to hook up, while their parents

How God Speaks

are someplace else, oblivious to the fact that their kids are about to lose their virginity, get pregnant, contract a venereal disease or two—or three. Funny how this never makes it into the movie.

In this episode the teens get to the cabin and settle in for some fun. Not a moment too soon, there is a rumble in the darkness outside. Tree limbs dance lazily in front of the camera as you begin to look through Jason's eyes. He peers at the unsuspecting teens through an open window. The scene is horror personified.

It's not long before the Jason music commences. It is both unmistakable and unforgettable, a signature of this horror series. "Chee, chee, chee, chee, chee, hau, hau, hau, hau, hau." Again and again the same refrain foreshadows eminent danger. It's not long before some "stupid" member of the group wanders through the dense darkness to the outhouse, in the dead of night, with no one around, to release his bowels. Of course, he ends up disemboweled, as Jason ends his camping trip for good.

In the succeeding scenes, Jason stalks the campers, seemingly aware of their every move, appearing around corners, behind trees, in the lake—everywhere. He seemed omnipresent.

That was enough for me. I watched the rest of that movie, but it wasn't something I was going to repeat. Even now I still remember those images, fixed in the back of my mind, like some bad dream. Therein lies the rub on entertainment that negatively alters the mind. My temple, God's chosen hangout spot, will never quite be the same.

In the Garden of Eden a similar metamorphosis happened. A sullen Adam and Eve were fresh off their meeting with Satan. Eve shivered for the first time in the cool of the day. Adam, sensing the weight of his guilt and sin, beckons Eve to the relative cover of a nearby bush, for this was the time of day when God would visit them.

On this day, however, there would be no hugs and kisses. There would be no sweet embraces, no long walk with the God who so loved to meet with them. Something had changed, and they could feel it. The air was chilled. The trees seemed to droop. Some of the animals looked at them with wild stares they had never seen before. Some of the birds flew close but never came to them as they had before.

The world had changed.

Suddenly they heard the sound of God walking to the spot where He always met them. The gentle steps that once signaled the presence of their Maker and King were now a thunderous thud. His voice bore no change, but to them it was as the sound of an angry river.

CAN YOU HEAR ME NOW?

With loving tones He called out to them, "Where are you?" (Genesis 3:9), but sinful ears no longer perceived love. Sin introduced into the life of created beings changes how they view their Creator.

Sin had changed their loving God into a stalker, brushing through the trees like some cosmic Jason, bent on their destruction.

To God's dismay, there was no answer at first. Finally He came to the spot where they were, and they could hide no more. With sadness in His eyes God saw His crowning creations cowering in the bushes.

That's when He hugged them as the tears rolled down their cheeks, and His. He knew there was a backup plan called salvation, but He'd hoped He would never have to use it. He knew they could no longer stay in the garden, that life for them and countless generations would have to be reborn.

But He loved them! They would be forgiven.

THE 411. . . . .

Read the account of the Fall in Genesis 3. Do you sometimes hide from God when you fall? Does your sin change the way you hear God? If you've ever felt like hiding, be comforted in this promise: "All that the Father gives me will come to me, and whoever comes to me I will never drive away" (John 6:37).

Gentle Whispers

"After the earthquake came a fire, but the Lord was not in the fire. And after the fire came a gentle whisper" (1 Kings 19:12).

We've learned this week that God has many ways of talking to His children. He relishes the chance to guide our footsteps in the way that they should go.

Today we will look at a familiar passage in 1 Kings 19, one that is both unsettling and comforting in times of distress and need.

"Elijah was afraid and ran for his life. When he came to Beersheba in Judah, he left his servant there, while he himself went a day's journey into the desert. He came to a broom tree, sat down under it and prayed that he might die. 'I have had enough, Lord,' he said. 'Take my life; I am no better than my ancestors.' Then he lay down under the tree and fell asleep.

"All at once an angel touched him and said, 'Get up and eat.' He looked around, and there by his head was a cake of bread baked over hot

How God Speaks

coals, and a jar of water. He ate and drank and then lay down again.

"The angel of the Lord came back a second time and touched him and said, 'Get up and eat, for the journey is too much for you.' So he got up and ate and drank. Strengthened by that food, he traveled forty days and forty nights until he reached Horeb, the mountain of God. There he went into a cave and spent the night.

"And the word of the Lord came to him: 'What are you doing here, Elijah?'

"He replied, 'I have been very zealous for the Lord God Almighty. The Israelites have rejected your covenant, broken down your altars, and put your prophets to death with the sword. I am the only one left, and now they are trying to kill me too.'

"The Lord said, 'Go out and stand on the mountain in the presence of the Lord, for the Lord is about to pass by.'

"Then a great and powerful wind tore the mountains apart and shattered the rocks before the Lord, but the Lord was not in the wind. After the wind there was an earthquake, but the Lord was not in the earthquake. After the earthquake came a fire, but the Lord was not in the fire. And after the fire came a gentle whisper. When Elijah heard it, he pulled his cloak over his face and went out and stood at the mouth of the cave.

"Then a voice said to him, 'What are you doing here, Elijah?'" (verses 3–13).

It's fair to say that Elijah is a bit traumatized. The evil Jezebel and her wicked husband, Ahab, are after Elijah for the massacre of the prophets of Baal on Mount Carmel just a few days earlier. Elijah not only mocked the false prophets; he summoned a divine blowtorch from heaven that licked up his water-drenched sacrifice.

The people spontaneously erupted in praise to God. "The Lord—he is God! The Lord—he is God!" (1 Kings 18:39). Then he had the people seize the prophets of Baal, take them down to a nearby valley, and slaughter them.

So Elijah had ample reason to run. Hidden in a mountain retreat, he begged God to take his life. He was tired of running. After a while God sent His angel to minister to Elijah in his distress, but Elijah continued in his depression.

Then came a mighty wind that tore the mountain apart and shattered the rocks. Elijah probably believed that God had accepted his prayer and was indeed going to kill him. But God was not in the wind. Then came a mighty earthquake followed by a massive fire, but God was in neither of them.

CAN YOU HEAR ME NOW?

Then came a gentle whisper, and there was God. What would have happened if Elijah had decided to help God out by committing suicide? What would he have missed?

When huge disasters happen, we have a tendency to read them as some rebuke from God, some divinely calibrated wake-up call. That's not necessarily true. Sometimes what we see are simply the workings of Satan. These events should lead us to listen deeper. After the winds of discouragement ease, the earthquakes and fiery trials cease, there we will find the immovable One. Hear ye Him.

THE 411. . . . .

Get a piece of paper and a pencil. Make a list of your greatest successes, times in your life when God helped you graduate from school, got you out of trouble, or helped you overcome a bad habit. What was that feeling like?

Now list some of the down moments in your life, times when you were at your lowest, emotionally and spiritually. Did you sense the presence of God? Why or why not?

No matter how great our triumphs or how deep our despair, God is always near.

CHAPTER 6

Sweet Lips!

Straight Talk

"How painful are honest words!" (Job 6:25).

I'm one of those people who like straight talk. I don't like people tip-toeing around me when they have something to say. If I've done something wrong, or right, I want to know about it, preferably from the one directly affected by my actions.

It is a policy that has landed me in some ticklish situations from time to time. Sometimes I have to address coworkers about their work. It's often difficult and sometimes downright grating, but I struggle through it with the belief that honesty is the framework on which all relationships are built. I also encourage my coworkers to take me to task when I slip up.

However, honesty, especially that which is delivered without tact or thoughtfulness, is not always the best policy. A few years ago I ran into an old friend I grew up with. We sat talking for a while, and then she interrupted our walk down memory lane with this statement: "Neil," she called me by my middle name, "you need to cut your nose hairs. Ooh, they are sticking out." She added a wide, boisterous laugh for good measure.

Although she was "my home girl" and we go way back, she didn't have to mention my nose hairs. I'm a little sensitive about that. Honest words spoken at the wrong time, well, they can change a great moment instantly.

Once I attended a church service and found myself in a serious predicament. The speaker had taken pains to put together a well-thought-out presentation on spiritualism and the occult. However, the presentation lacked any real in-depth focus on the Word of God.

Can You Hear Me Now?

As I sat listening, I was conscious of at least one new believer who had recently begun attending the church. She was truly searching for God, and this seemed like the kind of presentation that could encourage or complicate that search. At least this was my conclusion.

With each passing moment I grew more anxious. The presentation was titillating, sensational, and engaging. The only thing it lacked was "the Word." And that was a hole I just couldn't accept.

I felt like yelling out at the top of my voice, "When are you going to tell us how to insulate ourselves against Satan's attacks? How does God fit into this equation?"

At the end of the sermonette, time was given for questions. I turned to my wife and whispered, "I'm very bothered by any sermon that fails to include even one scripture." She could sense that I was upset, so she took hold of my hand and attempted to calm me.

I wasn't sure how to address the issue without attacking the speaker. My straight-talk policy had hit a snag. Sometimes it's OK to say what needs saying and let the chips fall where they may, but I had to consider whether my words would help or hurt the listeners. Furthermore, would God approve?

I decided to wait until a few other people had a chance to ask their questions. Then I raised my hand. The speaker recognized me.

I didn't preface my question with the usual "Thank you for your presentation; it was informative" statement. I couldn't bring myself to compliment the speaker. I was irate.

"Given what you have shared with us, what should Christians do to protect themselves from this kind of spiritualism?" He paused for a moment. I believe he felt the anger in my voice, though my question seemed harmless enough. His answer left me unconvinced, so I launched in again. "What role does God's Word play in helping Christians fortify themselves against attacks of the enemy?"

This time I spoke to what my deeper concern was, and the point was made. I felt that the service had been one long infomercial for Satan. I am certain that this was not the speaker's intention. He simply wanted to share with the audience some of the spiritualistic practices at work in our world. However, I wanted more.

After the service ended, I started to go ream him out, but I decided to hold my tongue. God had not appointed me "Enforcer of All Things Theological." "It's not your duty to set anyone straight," I could hear the Holy Spirit—and my wife—say.

82

Sweet Lips!

Instead, I chose to affirm him. I thanked him for sharing the information he did, and I expressed to him my conviction that the only safeguard in a world run by the prince of darkness is a deep abiding personal relationship with God and His Holy Word, the Bible. We hugged and departed.

The longer I live, the more I am learning that much more important than what we say is how and when we say what we say. For even honest words can be hurtful.

THE 411. . . . .

Have you injured someone with what you thought were honest words that needed to be spoken? What have you done to make things right with the person you wronged?

Perhaps someone has said something to you that was not very thoughtful. What should you do about it? Ask God for wisdom to use your speech with tact and grace.

The Iceman Cometh

"The words of the wise are like goads, their collected sayings like firmly embedded nails" (Ecclesiastes 12:11).

It was November and the snow was falling, as it often does during an early winter. It was the first major snowfall of the year in Philadelphia. You can always tell when the first winter snowstorm is under way. Eager television reporters don parkas, hats, and gloves and wait on every street corner counting each snowflake, carefully reporting their size and weight. The world could end, and there would be slightly a hiccup in the endless storm warnings.

The forecast said five to eight inches, which made my wife leap with excitement. My bride, a California transplant, has not quite lost the wonder of a snowfall. As soon as the first few flurries begin to dust the ground, the inevitable question arises.

"Dwain, can we go play in the snow?" This question is usually met with a shrug of silence. For me, snow is a beautiful nuisance that will complicate my life for the near future. For my wife, there is no such consideration.

"Sure, sweetheart," I less than enthusiastically respond. "Maybe later." At this a smile as big as an avalanche rushes over her face, like a 5-year-old child getting ready for her first snowball fight.

On this day the snow started early and fell all day. By evening there was seven inches on the ground, and since the crews had basically cleared the

Can You Hear Me Now?

major roadways, I decided to take a drive. I'd been cooped up for most of the day, so I was looking forward to a little fresh air. Boy, was that a bad move.

I drove about a block or so away from my home. The street that ran behind my home was not plowed very well, but I was undaunted. I would not be deterred. My rear-wheel-drive car was hardly a match for the hardening snow, but I kept on driving—and skidding.

At the very next corner I prepared to make a left onto a street that was fairly clear, except for the slushy mix at the corner. I pressed the accelerator, and the rear of the car began to dance, fishtailing wildly. That was my cue to let off the gas a little. I did, but before I knew it I was stuck, and no matter how hard I gunned the engine, the tires went nowhere but round and round.

Perhaps I'm trying to start off too fast, I reasoned. I decided to put the automatic transmission into the lowest gear. Again, no traction. I guess I looked pretty helpless, because a couple out walking their dog and enjoying the evening came over to offer their help.

"Can we give you a hand?" they asked.

"Sure," I responded. "It's really nice of you to do this," I noted. "You know, I don't live very far from here. I could just go home and grab a shovel. You really don't need to interrupt your walk." Silently I was glad they had stopped.

"That's no problem," the man said. "By the way, I'm Mark, and that's Christin," he pointed at his companion.

"I'm Dwain. Nice to meet you both."

After examining the situation, we decided that Christin would drive while we pushed. You couldn't really call what we did pushing, because the car went nowhere.

Mark then suggested that we get some tree branches from a nearby field and place them under the rear tires. It sounded like a good idea, so we trudged our way through the deep snow to a place where we found a few broken pine tree branches. We brought them back and tried moving the car again. It was futile. The tires simply spun out on the pine branches, perfuming the air with the smell of Pine-Sol.

I offered again to leave the car at the intersection and run home for a shovel. I was also a little concerned that Mark and Christin had interrupted their walk to help pull out a car that was hopelessly stuck. However, they seemed unwilling to leave me there.

We were all surprised when another visitor appeared out of nowhere. I hesitate to call this guy an angel, but he sure acted like one. He also had all the answers to my dilemma.

Sweet Lips!

"Can I give you a hand?" he offered. He wore a Sherlock Holmes overcoat, complete with a tie. The only things missing were the signature hat, pipe, and accent. He had to be an angel.

His name was also Mark. We all introduced ourselves and sized up my predicament once more.

"Why don't we try this?" he said. We all perked up at some fresh ingenuity. We had tried everything—and failed. "Why don't we push the car back a few yards and instead of trying to make a left turn here, which is slightly uphill, make a right and go downhill?"

His words seemed to make instant sense. We hadn't noticed that we had been trying desperately to get the car up a slight incline, something that would never be successful with the traction such as it was.

"OK," we said. "Let's try it." With Christin driving, we managed to roll the car back with little effort. The three of us men then walked to the back of the car and pushed it slightly. The car moved out from the quagmire without a single spin of the tires. It was frankly amazing.

"How did you know to do that, Mark?" I asked.

"Well, I grew up in New England, and you learn pretty quickly how to get around in this kind of weather," he said humbly, smiling. "I've been there before." He then pointed out some other roads that I could take to avoid getting stuck again, and with that he said goodbye and walked away.

I thanked Mark and Christin for their help, and then I drove off. I also thanked God for sending the Marks brothers and Christin to help me that night. There was no way I could have made it out of the snow on my own. Sometimes God sends just the right person with just the right words at just the right time.

Thank You, God.

THE 411. . . . .

The writer of Ecclesiastes likens the words of the wise to "firmly embedded nails." What do you think he meant? Can someone hang their actions on your words?

Living Water

"Whoever believes in me, as the Scripture has said, streams of living water will flow from within him" (John 7:38).

Ever wonder how Jesus was able to help so many for so long, yet never lose the light upbeat air that characterized His life? How did He continually encourage the depressed, heal the sick, free the demon-possessed, and raise the dead day after day without so much as a hint of disdain? I continue to be amazed by how positive Jesus was.

Day after day people would press in around Jesus. Many others traveled countless miles simply to catch a glimpse of Him. Some of them would pull and tug at His clothing, believing that one touch would forever heal them. And they were right.

Mothers would bring their babies to Him to be blessed. They had heard about how He always welcomed little children into His presence no matter how tired He was. A rumor of one incident made the rounds from city to city.

Once when the disciples grew tired of the children playing and tugging on Jesus, and them, they started to shoo them away. They even started to get upset at those who brought the little ones.

"Then little children were brought to Jesus for him to place his hands on them. But the disciples rebuked those who brought them.

"Jesus said, 'Let the little children come to me, and do not hinder them, for the kingdom of heaven belongs to such as these'" (Matthew 19:13, 14). The terse rebuke from Jesus must have caught the disciples off guard.

However, the following verse is really the kicker. "When he had placed his hands on them, he went on from there"(verse 15). Jesus refused to leave until He had blessed every child in sight. There is no record of how many children were there. Perhaps there were 20 or 50 or 150. Whatever the number, Jesus didn't really care. For Him time stood still.

There was something about the children that caught Jesus' undivided attention: They believed in Him. He could see in their eyes an innocent trust, a virgin calm in His presence.

And it wasn't only in the children's eyes. The people Jesus met with daily had become jaded by the religion of the Pharisees, Sadducees, and scholars of the law. They longed to believe in someone or something. In Jesus they got both.

He was a force, a freak of nature that carried around His own supply of oxygen. There was something about Him that set everyone who believed in Him at ease. The tone of His voice was soft yet commanding. His teachings were profound, yet simple enough for everyone to grasp. He excluded no one from His presence.

Those who were fortunate to see Him, hear Him, touch Him, were never the same. For He spoke words to their hearts. On one such occasion

Sweet Lips!

while attending the Feast of Tabernacles in Judea, Jesus looked out at the worshippers assembled, and He simply could not resist. They looked eagerly upon Him, awaiting each word as if drinking from a living cistern.

"Whoever believes in me, as the Scripture has said, streams of living water will flow from within him" (John 7:38). The disciple John goes on to clarify that Jesus spoke of the Holy Spirit, who would one day be poured out on all who believed in Jesus. When the people heard Jesus, it resonated with them, for they were beholding with their own eyes the Living Water of life.

If the water Jesus spoke about was anything like that which flowed out of Him, they had to have it.

THE 411. . . . .

Read John 4:1-26. What kind of water did Jesus want to give the woman who met Him at the well? How was the woman changed by her interaction with Jesus?

B-Nice

"He was a good man, full of the Holy Spirit and faith, and a great number of people were brought to the Lord" (Acts 11:24).

Ever been around a really good person? Someone who just seemed to be too good to be true, too good for this planet; someone who was really an angel in disguise, doing time on earth?

I know several people like that, and they've illuminated my spiritual journey. The names John and Donna Washington might not mean much to you, but I wish you could meet them. I met them when I first started working at the Review and Herald Publishing Association. They introduced themselves to me and my new bride at the time, Kemba. They were so thoughtful and kind that we started attending their church.

I remember once when Satan had gotten the best of me and I sat in my office discouraged, Donna called and left me a voice-mail message that I have never erased. The message was so affirming, so encouraging, so uplifting, that I knew it came directly from God. She is always there to give a word of advice when I'm spending too much time at work or having "wife trouble."

There are few people I know who would see something that matches the decor of our home and buy it for us. Donna Washington is one of

CAN YOU HEAR ME NOW?

those people. Her price is far above rubies.

Countless times I've walked to the book warehouse where John has his psychiatric practice. That's the only way to describe the quality of advice John dispenses to those who stop by—and they are many. It really doesn't matter the problem. His ear is always open, and he knows how to keep a secret. That's what I love about him.

Each day people come for a turn on his proverbial couch. When Kemba and I contemplated buying a new home, John was there to give us good counsel. He even went to the building site to be sure that the builders were not giving us the shaft. When we moved to Philadelphia, he helped us load the truck, drove it to Philadelphia, and helped us unpack it. We finished the night with the hardest job of all: unloading the piano. If you have a friend who is willing to help you move a piano, that's a true friend!

The Bible tells the story of someone who had a similar Midas touch with people. He was noble but down-to-earth, an angel hanging out on earth. And it didn't much matter whether he knew you or not. If you were fortunate enough to be in his presence, you felt elevated; you felt better.

His powers of encouragement were severely tested when a certain high-profile Christian tormentor became converted. The man was galloping gingerly atop his horse, riding to Damascus, a place where he would seek and destroy any followers of the recently crucified Jesus.

But something miraculous happened. While he was on the way, a flash of bright light knocked him from his horse and blinded him. Then came a voice from heaven, saying, "Saul, Saul, why do you persecute me?" Startled, Saul replied, "Who are you, Lord?" He knew it was God who had called him.

"'I am Jesus, whom you are persecuting,' he replied. 'Now get up and go into the city, and you will be told what you must do'" (Acts 9:4-6).

Paul's new conversion was not welcomed by those in the fledgling Christian church. In fact, when most heard about it they were very afraid. But Paul was undaunted. He preached with such power in the early days after his conversion that the Jewish leaders plotted to kill him. His followers had to smuggle him out of Damascus to Jerusalem.

When he got to Jerusalem he searched for some familiar faces, the infamous apostles of Jesus Christ. But his reputation preceded him. They would not meet with him for fear that he would turn state's evidence against them.

But one man took a chance on Paul. He saw in Paul a true conversion, and he decided to put his reputation on the line to get Paul accepted.

Sweet Lips!

The Bible says, "But Barnabas took him and brought him to the apostles. He told them how Saul on his journey had seen the Lord and that the Lord had spoken to him, and how in Damascus he had preached fearlessly in the name of Jesus" (verse 27).

Barnabas remained a lifelong friend of the great apostle Paul, accompanying him on many missionary excursions. He encouraged the other apostles to accept Paul. This act of Christian love is one of the most powerful acts in the entire Bible.

People felt really special around Barnabas. He made them feel loved and accepted. He lived out the true meaning of his name, "son of encouragement."

The 411. . . . .

Do you take time to make people feel accepted? How about those who may have done you wrong in the past? What does Barnabas' example of Christian love tell us about how we should treat all people?

Before You Go In

"In the fortieth year, on the first day of the eleventh month, Moses proclaimed to the Israelites all that the Lord had commanded him concerning them" (Deuteronomy 1:3).

"Are we there yet?"

"No."

"Are we there yet?"

"No."

Over and over the young children grilled their parents. "What's taking so long?" they questioned. "Someone said it takes only eight days to go from Mount Horeb to the Promised Land. You've been trying to get there since before we were born, right?"

By now the tired parents were growing even more tired with each smart comment. Truth is, the kids were right. The eight-day excursion had stretched into much more than a three-hour tour. They had been on the road for 40 years, to be exact. None of the original Israelite slaves from Egypt were around to experience the culmination of the journey.

From the east side of the Jordan River they could see Canaan, a beautiful land with lush, green expanses, bursting at the seams with fruits and vegetables they could never grow in the desert. This was the place

89

Can You Hear Me Now?

they had dreamed about, the shining star in a 40-year midnight of terror, most of which they had brought upon themselves.

But as the Israelites prepared to enter the Promised Land, Moses rose to his tired feet and quieted the crowd. The old man, worn by the trials of dealing with a hard-hearted and stiff-necked group, figured he'd take one last stab at reminding the people of their responsibility to God.

Moses was painfully aware that the generation entering the Promised Land was somewhat disconnected from their history. None of them had felt the lash of an Egyptian whip. None had known the fear of looking off in the distance and seeing Pharaoh's army beating a path through the desert in one final attempt to destroy the people of God. They'd heard the stories of the miraculous Red Sea deliverance, the first manna that fell from heaven, and the people who overate until it came out of their noses.

They had seen the cloud that guided them by day and the pillar of fire that lit up the night sky, but that was a "now" revelation. All they knew of the past were the stories they had been told.

With this in mind, Moses had a tall order ahead of him. The book of Deuteronomy is basically a transcript of Moses' special speech to the Israelites. It's a book of remembrance, and one that ought to be read and studied carefully.

Moses began by retelling the old story of the people's deliverance from Egypt and God's promise at Mount Horeb to give them a place they could call home. He told them of the many victories over numerous enemies. Moses waxed eloquently as he remembered the faithfulness of God.

The more he remembered the goodness of God, the more he exhorted the people to love God with every fiber of their being. Witness this beautiful passage: "Has any other people heard the voice of God speaking out of fire, as you have, and lived? Has any god ever tried to take for himself one nation out of another nation, by testings, by miraculous signs and wonders, by war, by a mighty hand and an outstretched arm, or by great and awesome deeds, like all the things the Lord your God did for you in Egypt before your very eyes?" (Deuteronomy 4:33, 34).

The people all nodded their approval. There was no other God who could have done such great things. Moses continued, describing just how special the land was that would soon be theirs.

"The land you are entering to take over is not like the land of Egypt, from which you have come, where you planted your seed and irrigated it by foot as in a vegetable garden. But the land you are crossing the Jordan to take possession of is a land of mountains and valleys that drinks rain from heaven.

Sweet Lips!

"It is a land the Lord your God cares for; the eyes of the Lord your God are continually on it from the beginning of the year to its end" (Deuteronomy 11:10-12).

Moses then implores his listeners by recounting one of the most beautiful passages in the Bible: "So if you faithfully obey the commands I am giving you today—to love the Lord your God and to serve him with all your heart and with all your soul—then I will send rain on your land in its season, both autumn and spring rains, so that you may gather in your grain, new wine, and oil" (verses 13, 14).

The formula was simple: obey and prosper. But far more than that, what God craved most was love. That's all He ever wanted from their foreparents, and that's all He would ever require of them.

Moses' words introduced a new generation to an old God whose mercies were new every day. The God who gave them the Promised Land would also protect and prosper their every work—if they obeyed Him. Moses' words set just the right tone for Israel's sojourn in Canaan. He reminded them of God's love.

Don't you wish we had a few more folks like Moses around?

THE 411. . . . .

If someone wanted you to tell them about God based on your past experiences about Him, what would you say? What experiences have changed your life the most?

Now try this. Call up a friend and share your special story.

They Said What?

"Timothy, guard what has been entrusted to your care. Turn away from godless chatter and the opposing ideas of what is falsely called knowledge" (1 Timothy 6:20).

Nobody's perfect, right? We all wish we had the perfect shape or the perfect job or the perfect mate. If one looks long enough, there is always something that can be remade, improved, bettered.

I particularly admire people who have the unique ability to rattle off articulate, grammatically bulletproof sentences at the drop of a hat. I have watched Secretary of State Colin Powell hold court at a few State Department briefings. He not only manages to be articulate, but does so with humor and rhetorical flourish.

CAN YOU HEAR ME NOW?

Another wordsmith is Secretary of Defense Donald Rumsfeld. Watching his briefings with the media is a study in sentence structure. More than one reporter has felt the verbal assault of a carefully worded Rumsfeld rebuke. Many people, political junkies like me especially, check C-SPAN each day to see what Rumsfeld said. Plain and simple, he's entertaining.

But for all the articulate spokespersons in the Bush administration, George W. Bush struggles when asked to make comments on the fly. During his first campaign for the presidency Bush noted in a speech, "[I want to] make sure everybody who has a job wants a job." Touting his "No Child Left Behind" education policy, Bush noted, "Rarely is the question asked: Is our children learning?"

While some have concluded—erroneously—from such snafus that Bush lacks the "gray matter" to be president, others would gladly trade Bill Clinton's White House escapades for Bush's verbal nonprowess.

Verbal snafus aside, every human being comes out of the womb with a budding desire to be understood. Some of us just have a harder time getting our point across than others. Consider, for instance, Yogi Berra, former manager of the Dodgers and the person who has elevated misstatement to an art form. He is widely credited with first uttering, "It ain't over till it's over."

Berra is also reported to have said, "You can observe a lot by just watching," which is true. Witness this Yogi-ism: "You've got to be careful if you don't know where you're going, because you might not get there"; or this one: "Baseball is 90 percent mental—the other half is physical." Berra's warmth and genuine spirit transcend his words, giving them meaning.

Words are but a small percentage of the communication we give each day. Our words are surrounded by gestures, looks, sounds, etc., that deepen and extend the meaning of what we say. Even when we make a flub, those listening and looking at us can mine our communication for more input that makes the meaning clear.

Further, they can draw on a reservoir of time spent with us. They know we are generally good people. Even strangers tend to have a belief in the general goodness of the person to whom they are talking.

However, there are people whose speech betrays them. No matter how much we give them the benefit of the doubt, the content of what they are saying overshadows everything. When President Bush utters one of his patented Bushisms, we write it off because we have a general belief that our president meant well.

That's not the kind of person the apostle Paul was warning young

Sweet Lips!

Timothy against. Evidently Timothy was ministering at a time when people were carrying a cloak of philosophy and learning, even as they refused to utter a single word about God.

Paul warned young Timothy to stay clear of "godless chatter." Certainly he was concerned that such "enlightened" conversation was not really enlightened at all. The same is true today. People enjoy talking about just about everything except God. Don't believe it? Try starting a conversation about God with your neighbors.

As Christians we are called to speak a different language, to communicate a different message, one that is never to be mixed with the "wisdom" of the world.

THE 411. . . . .

Read Paul's charge to Timothy found in 1 Timothy 6. What else does Paul warn Timothy about? Why?

What are some of the modern-day temptations that can affect our ministry for God?

Union With Christ

"A word aptly spoken is like apples of gold in settings of silver" (Proverbs 25:11).

Jesus Christ goes on the record. There's been a mountain of ink spilled trying to explain the words of Jesus, but none quite match the power and majesty of Jesus' own words. He spoke these words to His disciples and to us. We are inextricably linked with Jesus Christ, and that's great news.

I am the true vine,
and My Father is the vinedresser.

Every branch in Me that does not bear fruit,
He takes away; and every branch that bears fruit,
He prunes it, that it may bear more fruit.

You are already clean
because of the word which I have
spoken to you.

CAN YOU HEAR ME NOW?

Abide in Me, and I in you.
As the branch cannot bear fruit of itself,
unless it abides in the vine,
so neither can you,
unless you abide in Me.

I am the vine, you are the branches;
he who abides in Me, and I in him, he bears much fruit;
for apart from Me you can do nothing.

If anyone does not abide in Me,
he is thrown away as a branch, and dries up;
and they gather them,
and cast them into the fire,
and they are bound.

If you abide in Me,
and My words abide in you,
ask whatever you wish,
and it shall be done for you.

By this is My Father glorified,
that you bear much fruit,
and so prove to be My disciples.

Just as the Father has loved Me,
I have also loved you; abide
in My love.

If you keep My commandments,
you will abide in My love;
just as I have kept My Father's
commandments,
and abide in His love.

—John 15:1-10, NASB

THE 411.

We can't do anything without Jesus. We can't make any positive changes if He does not give us the power to do so. But no matter how much Jesus can do for us, we must give Him permission to come into our hearts.

CHAPTER 7

When God Speaks

Now

"A time to tear and a time to mend, a time to be silent and a time to speak" (*Ecclesiastes 3:7*).

When does God speak? Are there special circumstances that compel Him to butt into our business, or, even more than that, announce His intentions beforehand? What moves God to chatter at some moments and not at others?

I must confess I'd often wondered about this strange trait of God until a light went on in my brain after a certain experience I had.

The year was 2001. My wife and I were relocating to Philadelphia, Pennsylvania, and frankly, we didn't know where we were going to live. It was one of those "Lord, we've got a problem so You've got a problem" moments.

We searched endlessly for just the right place, but every time we settled on one, it would be under contract or sold before we even had a chance to see it. It was a nightmare.

Miraculously, God blessed us with an older home in a very nice neighborhood. One day my wife happened to be walking through the West Mount Airy section of the city. She actually went there to see a home that had come on the market. One look at the weathered exterior, the bathroom built into the living room, and the water-damaged ceilings, and there was no way we were going to sink money into that place.

She kept on walking in the same area when she noticed another house for sale on Lincoln Drive, one of the really nice streets on the outskirts of

Can You Hear Me Now?

Philadelphia. It's fairly rare to see a home on Lincoln Drive for sale. Most homeowners know the value of the area and rarely sell.

We quickly put in a bid on the Lincoln Drive house, and it was accepted. Shortly after we did, several other bids came in that were significantly higher than ours. But we had the contract. It was truly a miracle. People continue to marvel at the price we paid for our home.

We thanked God immensely for this blessing and asked Him to use our home to be a blessing to the entire neighborhood.

After filling out a gazillion forms (as anyone who has ever bought a home can testify), we prepared for closing. During the closing meeting I felt impressed to say a prayer of thanks to God at the end, but I was afraid.

I wasn't sure what faith the other people there belonged to. They certainly weren't Seventh-day Adventists. The real estate agent was a Christian, but not of my faith. The seller's representative had been trying to break our contract in the days leading up to the close, so that he could take a higher bid. Surely he wouldn't want to hear anything about praying. In addition, our lawyer, a pit bull of a woman who fought hard so we wouldn't be taken advantage of, didn't seem to be in the mood for anything spiritual.

But the voice grew louder. "I am the One who blessed you. You really should say a prayer of thanks so that everyone involved can know that I am the One who blessed you."

I decided to obey. The moment of truth came. All the documents were signed, and everyone prepared to leave. That's when I interrupted them.

"May I have your attention for a moment?" I asked. Everyone turned around, no doubt worried that perhaps I had changed my mind. I continued.

"I hope you don't mind, but my wife and I are Christians. We believe that God is the one who gave us this home, and if you don't mind, I'd like to say a prayer of thanks to Him, and I'd like to thank Him for each person's contribution to this meeting." The group gathered around the large conference table warily.

Everyone in the room was stunned, but pleasantly so, I thought. At that moment I lifted a heartfelt prayer to God, thanking Him for each person in the room and the gift of our home. I asked Him to bless our home so that it would be a light in the Mount Airy community. Then we said amen.

Several people thanked me for the prayer and talked about how special the moment was. I felt at peace, as though I had heard the voice of

96

When God Speaks

God speaking directly to me and for once I had obeyed. I felt spiritually elevated. They didn't notice, but I was gliding.

THE 411. . . . .

When does God speak? He speaks whenever there is an opportunity to tell someone about Him. What I learned was this: God is constantly speaking to me. However, I am not always tuned in to hear Him.

Today, look for chances to share Jesus with someone. Then look out. God is going to tell you just what to do.

Caught!

" 'No one, sir,' she said. 'Then neither do I condemn you,' Jesus declared. 'Go now and leave your life of sin' " (John 8:11).

Is there a more beautiful scripture in the Bible than the one you just read? I don't think there is. This verse is one of the most quoted in the Bible, and for good reason.

It is the culmination of a dark episode in the life of a nameless woman. The Bible writers must have forgotten to mention her name, or more likely, her behavior was so revolting that her name was not worthy of print. Whatever the case, she forever wears the nondescript, generic moniker of the "woman caught in adultery."

Her predicament was dire. In the Middle Eastern culture of her time women didn't fare well. Men had a final say in every facet of a woman's life. She was expected to care for the home, perhaps sow and harvest crops with her children in the field, and fetch water for the animals. It was a long, grueling life. Some men valued their animals more than they did their wives. Life wasn't easy for women.

It follows then that someone with such low status had very little protection from the law, since—you guessed it—men wrote the laws. At the time, adultery was a capital offense punishable by death to the woman. The man was to be punished equally, but this was hardly the case.

Author Ellen G. White writes, "With all their professions of reverence for the law, these rabbis, in bringing the charge against the woman, were disregarding its provisions. It was the husband's duty to take action against her, and the guilty parties were to be punished equally. The action of the accusers was wholly unauthorized" (*The Desire of Ages,* p. 461).

The system of punishment was by no means fair or equitable. That is

CAN YOU HEAR ME NOW?

what made Jesus' response to this moral crisis so earthshaking. Jesus was about to overturn hundreds of years of Jewish law, and He didn't even flinch. How many of us would have the guts to stand in the middle of an angry jury of our peers and declare a murderer free to go and sin no more? That's sort of what Jesus did. The crime of adultery carried the stigma and abhorrence that murder does today.

Yet our Lord was undaunted by the odds against Him. There was a good chance that His intervention could cause His own death. Remember, the woman was dragged before Jesus in a failed attempt to trap Him.

The Pharisees and scribes had trotted out the Law of Moses, which allowed but one cure for the disease of adultery—death. They wanted to know what Jesus thought, since He seemed to have no regard for their laws.

But Jesus saw in the woman's plight an opportunity to make a statement on the one need that we all have—to be forgiven.

As He bent down in the sand, calmly writing the names of the woman's accusers and each sin they had committed, Jesus was sending a message to all future generations. He seems to say, "I know that the one you brought to Me is worthy of condemnation, but so are you. I take no special pleasure in seeing sinful people destroyed, and neither should you—especially given the sins you are committing."

Jesus felt compelled to save the adulterous woman, and His quiet rebuke of the Pharisees and scribes was an opportunity for them to be saved.

THE 411. . . . .

In pardoning the woman caught in adultery, some would charge Jesus with going soft on sin. Not so, writes Ellen G. White. "In His act of pardoning this woman and encouraging her to live a better life, the character of Jesus shines forth in the beauty of perfect righteousness. While He does not palliate sin, nor lessen the sense of guilt, He seeks not to condemn, but to save" (*The Desire of Ages,* p. 462).

Unmistakable!

"And his sheep follow him because they know his voice" (John 10:4).

If you ever have the chance to observe sheep, you will soon recognize their dependability on the shepherd. Sheep will follow their master anywhere. However, a stranger has very little chance of budging them.

Even if you were somehow able to blindfold the sheep, none of them

When God Speaks

would be cajoled, tempted, or wooed into following an unfamiliar voice. Sheep are just too "simple" for such shenanigans. It is this simplicity, this dependency on the shepherd for everything, including life itself, that makes them most like us. Below is the Bible passage that links us forever with sheep.

" 'I tell you the truth, the man who does not enter the sheep pen by the gate, but climbs in by some other way, is a thief and a robber. The man who enters by the gate is the shepherd of his sheep. The watchman opens the gate for him, and the sheep listen to his voice. He calls his own sheep by name and leads them out.

" 'When he has brought out all his own, he goes on ahead of them, and his sheep follow him because they know his voice. But they will never follow a stranger; in fact, they will run away from him because they do not recognize a stranger's voice.'

"Jesus used this figure of speech, but they did not understand what he was telling them.

"Therefore Jesus said again, 'I tell you the truth, I am the gate for the sheep. All who ever came before me were thieves and robbers, but the sheep did not listen to them. I am the gate; whoever enters through me will be saved. He will come in and go out, and find pasture. The thief comes only to steal and kill and destroy; I have come that they may have life, and have it to the full.

" 'I am the good shepherd. The good shepherd lays down his life for the sheep. The hired hand is not the shepherd who owns the sheep. So when he sees the wolf coming, he abandons the sheep and runs away. Then the wolf attacks the flock and scatters it. The man runs away because he is a hired hand and cares nothing for the sheep.

" 'I am the good shepherd; I know my sheep and my sheep know me— just as the Father knows me and I know the Father—and I lay down my life for the sheep. I have other sheep that are not of this sheep pen. I must bring them also. They too will listen to my voice, and there shall be one flock and one shepherd' " (John 10:1-16).

When God speaks, His voice is unmistakable, and those who know it follow Him.

The 411 . . . .

Sheep learn to recognize the shepherd's voice from the time spent with the shepherd. How long does it take for us to recognize and know God's voice? Does the Holy Spirit play a role in this process?

Hunger Pains

"Then Jesus declared, 'I am the bread of life. He who comes to me will never go hungry, and he who believes in me will never be thirsty'" (John 6:35).

She was happy by most accounts, going about her life like most. She wasn't deeply spiritual, but she did believe in God. It wasn't that she never intended to give her heart to God, to make Him an integral part of her life; she just never got around to it.

She saw this decision as less consequential, partly because her father seemed to have enough spirituality for both of them combined. He attended church regularly and was loved by the other church members who knew him well. He told anyone within earshot just what a great difference God had made in his life. He also tried not to miss any chance to share the love of Jesus with his daughter.

Whenever he prepared to leave his home, he would always carry little sharing books with him. These he would give to coworkers, friends, relatives, and people he ran into from day to day. The book he enjoyed giving most was the short inspirational book called *Steps to Christ*.

The books were stamped with the address of his church in Montclair, New Jersey, just in case someone was looking for a church home. It probably never crossed his mind that this simple book would save someone he loved dearly.

One day the phone at the church rang, and a frantic, tearful voice said hello.

"Is this the Montclair Seventh-day Adventist Church?" she asked.

"Yes," the warm voice responded.

"Can I talk to the pastor?" she requested.

"Sure." Arrangements were made for the young woman to speak with the pastor.

"Hello; how may I help you?" the pastor reassured.

"Well, sir, I just wanted to know more about your church," the woman began. She was obviously hurting, so the pastor was clearly concerned.

"My father died suddenly," she cried, "and I'm not sure what to do. When my father died, the only thing he had on him was a book called *Steps to Christ*. It was stamped with the address to your church."

The pastor listened intently, offering his condolences and prayers as she relayed the story to him.

"It's the only thing of his I have left. It's the only thing he left me," she

When God Speaks

continued. "I want what my father had. Can you tell me how to find God?"

The pastor listened quietly, moved by the deep spiritual hunger he heard in the woman's voice. "We'd be glad to help you find God," the pastor chimed in. Soon a time was set up for her to come in and speak with him.

In our world today there are countless people hungering and thirsting for food that only Jesus can give. You see them everywhere. Some know there's something missing in their lives; others go on their merry way, oblivious to their spiritual condition.

Sometimes God is forced to use any means available to save us. After my friend shared with me the story above, I wondered, *Did God allow her father to die so that He could save her?* On that note, let me assure you that God is not running around trying to kill people in an effort to save others. That's not how God operates. However, I do believe that God uses Satan's acts of destruction for His good.

Often one of the moments in life when God chooses to speak is during the pain and degradation of tragedy and loss. Odd timing, perhaps, but not to God. He sees in life's challenges an opportunity to give us the most important gift this side of heaven—Himself.

THE 411. . . . .

Read Deuteronomy 6:10-12 and answer the following questions: Who is doing the speaking in this verse? What is his message? Why do we forget God when everything is going well?

Why not give God your life now?

Special Words

"The Sovereign Lord has given me an instructed tongue, to know the word that sustains the weary" (Isaiah 50:4).

Wouldn't it be nice to know the right thing to say at the right time—all the time? Not some empty phrase or vacant platitude; this is "the" absolute best word, the one sent down from heaven, designed by God to meet the need of some specific soul. That's the kind of word I needed when I first got the bad news.

It happened on Sunday, but my dad shared it with me early the next morning. I had called to tell my parents the ghastly news about my brother-in-law. He had been in a terrible accident and was in desperate need of prayer.

I was doing what had become rote for me. Whenever there's a situation that seems unusually overwhelming, I call my parents. Such as the time when a newly baptized friend lost her job just two weeks after her baptism.

I remember calling my mother late one night to ask her to pray for this friend. I was especially concerned because my friend had been really searching to know God, and when she finally accepted Jesus as her Savior, the rug seemed to get pulled out from under her.

It was unsettling, but my mother—she of the silver tongue—knew just what to say.

"Son, God knows what He is doing," she began. "He will work this situation out. Satan doesn't want us to make any decisions that hurt his kingdom. God will be with your friend. I will ask God to give her strength to stand for Him, and provide her with new employment."

Nothing earth-shattering there, now that I think about it. But those words took on a special meaning when my mother spoke them. They had a depth that must have come from years of watching God work out difficult problems.

I try not to bother my parents with "my car had a flat tire" scenarios. Those I can handle on my own. But that day I needed more.

Before I could tell him about my brother-in-law, my father began to speak, his voice cracking. "Neil"—he calls me by my middle name—"I have some . . . bad . . . news for you."

Just what I need, I thought, *more bad news.* I wasn't expecting what came next.

"Your grandmother," he paused as he began to cry. "Your grandmother is dead. She died yesterday," he said, sobbing.

At that moment I wasn't sure how to respond. I didn't know what to say. I could count on two fingers the times I had heard my father in such agony. This was the second time. The first was when his father died.

I had seen my father cry before, as he did at my wedding, but this was different. This was cold, raw pain, and I wasn't sure how to relate.

What does one say to their father at a moment like this? Isn't he the one who always has the answers, who knows just the right encouragement to give? Shouldn't he know what to say to himself?

"Daddy, I'm so sorry," I hesitatingly offered. Unable to say anything else, I listened as he wept and talked about her.

As I listened to my father, I thought of what his mother meant to him. His father separated from her early in his life, so this was the woman who raised him. She was the one who cooked his favorite meals, taught him

When God Speaks

how to be a man and how to love. He owes much of who he is to her.

The hurt my father felt was made even more painful because he had been unable to visit his mother for several years (she resided on another continent). He never had the chance to say goodbye.

There are moments in life when words fail, washed away in a sea of agony and pain. It is at those precise moments that we grope around in the human lexicon for the supernatural, something that is not of this world. Such healing words can come from only one source, and that source is God.

When I ran out of words to comfort my father, God was just beginning to speak.

THE 411. . . . .

How do you reach out to friends or family who lose loved ones to death? Read Isaiah 50. Why did God give Isaiah an "instructed tongue"? How did he use it?

The Happy Hugger

"You shall not bow down to them or worship them; for I, the Lord your God, am a jealous God, punishing the children for the sin of the fathers to the third and fourth generation of those who hate me" (Exodus 20:5).

Jealousy is not exactly an admirable trait. Be honest. Who likes to be around someone who hangs all over their girlfriend like a leach, not to mention the fact that they probably shouldn't be draped all over them?

I remember a couple in my high school that seemed to be Siamese twins. You rarely ever saw one without the other, and it wasn't just that they enjoyed each other's company. At times it seemed that if they were separated and someone of the opposite sex spoke to one of them, a homing signal would go off and, boom, the other would mysteriously appear. They seemed to have some kind of ESP. After a while the rest of the school just seemed to give up on making contact with them. They were from another planet anyway.

Then there was the time when I attended a local church, which shall remain nameless. I was caught off guard by the way one of the deacons greeted the female members as they entered the church. I knew him very well. He was a really nice person, but as he approached my wife and me I got a little antsy.

His preferred method of greeting was not a handshake, not a "Happy

103

CAN YOU HEAR ME NOW?

Sabbath; great to see you." No, this guy believed in the holy hug. He was an older dude, with huge hands and what can only be described as a major gut. When he hugged a woman, he pulled her close, locking his huge arms around her back, and enveloping her body so that her spine curved around his huge stomach. All the air in her had to be squeezed out. What's more, he held her in that position for what seemed like an eternity.

All around us were women whose backs were slightly bowed from the ferocity and general perversion of the greeting. I'm exaggerating a bit here, but not much. He was hugger extraordinaire. He was the all-time embrace champion.

After a while I got the distinct feeling that this guy was getting the jollies out of his job. *Didn't he get enough attention from his wife?* I wondered. Come to think of it, I don't remember him being married.

Right before he hugged my wife, he put a stranglehold on a local pastor's wife that was positively sinful. After that one I was sure. This was no welcome to the house of God.

I thought about intercepting him as he approached, but that, I thought, wouldn't look right. It would be obvious that I had a problem with him "welcoming" my wife.

So I did what any other man in my position would do: I tried to avoid the situation. *When direct action seems fraught with danger, there's nothing better than a little avoidance. I can fight this battle next Sabbath,* I reasoned.

But avoidance would not work this day. He walked up to us, hugged me warmly—that much I appreciated—and proceeded to assault my wife. I felt violated as I walked away with a hunched-over Kemba at my side.

That morning at church the green-eyed monster got the best of me. I never doubted my wife's love. He wasn't going to take her from me in some *Gone With the Wind* saga of lost love. What upset me was the idea that someone seemed to be stealing privileges that belonged solely to me. My wife's body belongs to me, and mine belongs to her. No one is allowed to violate that bond in any way.

This might be a stretch, but I think God feels the same way about us. What's more, He doesn't like to share us with anyone. God is jealous about His place in our lives. He wants to be number one, everything, all, and when we attempt to replace Him He doesn't just walk away as I did after the hugger laid one on Kemba. Sooner or later He will let us know who is really number one.

When we replace God with other gods, we attract His attention.

104

When God Speaks

THE 411. . . . .

Read Exodus 34:11-17. What specific instructions did God give His people concerning how they are to relate with other nations? Why?

No Words

"He was oppressed and afflicted, yet he did not open his mouth; he was led like a lamb to the slaughter, and as a sheep before her shearers is silent, so he did not open his mouth" (Isaiah 53:7).

If you want to be changed, spend each day for two weeks reading Matthew 26-28. You will be transformed. Recently I began reading these chapters consistently after a friend encouraged me to examine seriously the closing scenes of Jesus' life. (It didn't hurt that *The Passion of the Christ* movie was really big at the time.)

One cannot help being struck by the plotting of the chief priests, Judas' kiss of betrayal, and the denials of Jesus' "boys," the disciples. These accounts leave you breathless.

However, neatly hidden among them is a rich gem that bears revealing. As you read the following passage, transport yourself there.

Picture the angry mob gathered around Pilate's judgment hall, the priests laying out the case against Jesus, whose face has become gaunt and sad amid the strain of your sins and mine. See Him shackled and in pain, the Creator tormented by His creatures.

"Now Jesus was standing before Pilate, the Roman governor. 'Are you the Jews' Messiah?' the governor asked him.

" 'Yes,' Jesus replied.

"But when the chief priests and other Jewish leaders made their many accusations against him, Jesus remained silent.

" 'Don't you hear what they are saying?' Pilate demanded.

"But Jesus said nothing, much to the governor's surprise.

"Now the governor's custom was to release one Jewish prisoner each year during the Passover celebration—anyone they wanted. This year there was a particularly notorious criminal in jail named Barabbas, and as the crowds gathered before Pilate's house that morning he asked them, 'Which shall I release to you—Barabbas, or Jesus your Messiah?' For he knew very well that the Jewish leaders had arrested Jesus out of envy because of his popularity with the people.

105

CAN YOU HEAR ME NOW?

"Just then, as he was presiding over the court, Pilate's wife sent him this message: 'Leave that good man alone; for I had a terrible nightmare concerning him last night.'

"Meanwhile the chief priests and Jewish officials persuaded the crowds to ask for Barabbas' release, and for Jesus' death. So when the governor asked again, 'Which of these two shall I release to you?' the crowd shouted back their reply: 'Barabbas!'

" 'Then what shall I do with Jesus, your Messiah?' Pilate asked.

"And they shouted, 'Crucify him!'

" 'Why?' Pilate demanded. 'What has he done wrong?' But they kept shouting, 'Crucify! Crucify!'

"When Pilate saw that he wasn't getting anywhere, and that a riot was developing, he sent for a bowl of water and washed his hands before the crowd, saying, 'I am innocent of the blood of this good man. The responsibility is yours!'

"And the mob yelled back, 'His blood be on us and on our children!' " (Matthew 27:11-25, TLB).

It's really hard to conceive that Jesus didn't say a word in His own defense. Most good defense lawyers never allow their clients to take the stand, lest they incriminate themselves during cross-examination by the prosecution. But Jesus had no legal counsel. He was all alone.

Pilate, the Roman governor at the time, seemed to sympathize with Jesus for a moment, giving Jesus a chance to defend Himself. To his chagrin, Jesus refused to talk. He said nothing. He was charged with impersonating God, a charge He could have easily disproved. All He needed to do was cause a great fire to engulf His accusers and more than likely He would have been released on the spot.

But Jesus understood His mission. This was His destiny, and there was no way that He was going to delay the show. The very people condemning Him to die needed His salvation. If any of them had a change of heart later and needed a Savior, the righteous, sinless life of Jesus lay on the record books of heaven.

Just how did Jesus do it? How did He endure it all without uttering a single word?

He who spoke up for the homeless, the demon-possessed, the sick, the helpless, could no longer hear a single comforting word from His Father. He had become sin for us. He loaded up a sack filled with your sins and mine and toted it up to the cross, where He paid for our freedom with His blood.

106

When God Speaks

The God who spoke the world into being uttered not a word so that He might save us. What is that gem worth to you?

THE 411. . . . .

Talk to Jesus right now. Tell Him what you think about His sacrifice. Ask Him to tell you what ran through His mind as He listened to the charges against Him. Ask Him if He saw you.

CHAPTER 8

Weird Godspeak

Wham!

"Now a man came up to Jesus and asked, 'Teacher, what good thing must I do to get eternal life?'" (Matthew 19:16).

We've all heard people say strange things before. Once when I happened to be walking down one of the aisles at a Wal-Mart Supercenter, I overheard a conversation. No, I wasn't being nosy. I think the speaker took a certain relish in the fact that everyone within a 20-mile radius could hear what he was saying.

He was talking to a rather old woman. She looked to be in her 70s. She was dressed in worn-out sweatpants, her hair was matted, and her face looked like the last rose of summer, as one friend's mother used to say. As she hunched over her cart in front of the loquacious one, I could tell that she was sucking up his every word like a vacuum cleaner.

"Honey"—his voice was dripping with sticky lies—"you look great! I think you're into your third childhood, girl!" he continued.

Undaunted by the picture of ill health in front of him, he kept up his tired rap: "I think you done turned the clock back, girl! You are lookin' good," he said, a huge cheesy grin on his weathered brow.

Finally the woman seemed to catch on to him, so in an effort to stem the tide of syrup washing over her, she said, "Well, I sure feel old. I got pains everywhere!"

Her words were scarcely out of her mouth when they were met with "Sweetheart, don't worry about those aches and pains. That's just letting you know you're alive, honey. You still got it!"

108

Weird Godspeak

The words of this huckster hit my ear with the subtlety of a sledge-hammer. *What's he trying to do?* I thought to myself. *Isn't it better to tell the truth at all times, and if you can't say something that is true, shouldn't you not say anything at all?* After I thought about it for a while, I realized that I was being too hard on the Wal-Mart Don Juan. He was trying to make a senior citizen feel good, to take her mind off of the challenges that come with growing older. It was a noble effort, if somewhat poorly executed.

People say crazy stuff. That's expected. They're just people. Who hasn't said a few stupid things from time to time? But what about God? Does God ever say things that don't make sense? Absolutely.

If you read the story of the rich young playboy in Matthew 19, you quickly come upon weird Godspeak. The first whack from the mouth of Jesus comes when the young man refers to Him as good. Jesus replies, "Why do you ask me about what is good? There is only One who is good" (verse 17). You cannot help wondering, *Did Jesus wake up on the wrong side of the bed that morning? Isn't He supposed to be nice? That didn't seem like a cool thing to say.*

But it doesn't stop there. Jesus continues: "If you want to enter life, obey the commandments." Now, wait one minute. Isn't it true that there's nothing we can "do" to earn eternal life? Isn't it the gift of God, through Jesus Christ? Why then does Jesus seem to encourage our resident playboy to work his way to heaven?

"Which ones?" the young man retorts. Now, you gotta give Jesus cool points, because in this question we see a little of what made Jesus respond to the young ruler as He did earlier. The young playboy was not really ready to give his all to God; he was looking to do the minimum required to get into heaven. Know anybody like that?

Jesus plays along with him for the moment. He lists several commandments: "Do not murder, do not commit adultery, do not steal, do not give false testimony, honor your father and mother, and love your neighbor as yourself" (verses 18, 19)—the latter covering all the commandments.

Ever wonder why Jesus didn't list all the commandments? For instance, why didn't He mention the first four commandments, the ones that deal with our relationship to God? The final six deal with our relationship to our fellow human beings, and He didn't even mention the last one of those: Thou shalt not covet anything that is thy neighbor's. Weird stuff, right?

"All these I have kept," the young man noted (verse 20). "What am I missing?" Here is where Jesus slams him really hard: "If you want to be perfect, go, sell your possessions and give to the poor, and you will have

CAN YOU HEAR ME NOW?

treasure in heaven. Then come, follow me" (verse 21).

The next verse the Bible records is one of the saddest in all of Scripture: "When the young man heard this, he went away sad, because he had great wealth" (verse 22). Unable to part with his treasures, the rich young ruler lost out on heaven.

In defense of Jesus it must be said that He discerned the spiritual condition of the young ruler at the very moment He saw him. From his rich clothing, his careful grooming, his noble bearing, and his fake humility, Jesus perceived that there was but one way to get this guy's attention. He had to jar him out of his comfort zone, much like a lawyer cross-examining a smooth but untruthful witness.

"Why do you ask about what is good?" was not the answer he expected from Jesus when he approached Him. I believe this was the first salvo that got his attention. Jesus' strategy of dealing with Mr. Bigbucks was further vindicated by the young ruler's inability to grasp the need to keep all of God's commandments. Notice, Jesus doesn't mention the first four commandments, which deal with a relationship to God, and the rich young ruler never seems to miss them. Can you guess why? He had no relationship with God!

Jesus looked past his appearance and straight into his heart. There was something blocking the rich young ruler's salvation, and Jesus put His finger on it when He told him to sell all that he had and give it to the poor. Instead of mentioning "Thou shalt not covet" among the commandments, Jesus tailor-made a commandment that tested him on this very point. There was a method to Jesus' "madness."

There always is.

THE 411. . . . .

The rich young ruler missed out on a golden chance to walk with Jesus. We know that Jesus' request was a stiff challenge to the young playboy, but why didn't he place more importance on the opportunity to follow Jesus? What prevents you from following Jesus?

It's Theirs
"Blessed are the poor in spirit, for theirs is the kingdom of heaven" (Matthew 5:3).

Ever watch the State of the Union address given each January by the president of the United States? In recent years this speech has started to in-

110

Weird Godspeak

terest me more and more. The president is tasked with giving the people a sort of report card on how things are going.

In all the years that I've watched this speech, the state of the union has never been weak, poor, challenged, or struggling. The president of the moment rattles off a litany of accomplishments: cut spending here, cut taxes there, conquered this "evil" enemy or that, strengthened the booming economy, etc. From one year to the next, very little seems to change. Inevitably, the state of the nation is sound, strong, robust, and poised for success.

To be sure, there are nodding winks to problems we still face. The ongoing terrorist threat to our shores keeps us all scared to death and on our toes, allowing the government more power to do whatever they think necessary to protect us. No matter what the challenge, we are assured by the commander in chief that we can face it down and win. The state of the nation is always strong and getting stronger.

I've often wondered how the words of our president strike the ears of those who are struggling to make ends meet in our society, to say nothing of the world. How does the father working three jobs to provide for his children interpret those words? What about the mother on welfare who wants to work but has no one to care for her children during the day, or no means of getting a job that pays a living wage? Do these people come to the same conclusion as the president?

The ones who are broken by the challenges of their lives—how does it hit them? I remember growing up in East Orange, New Jersey. I remember my mother paying for our groceries with food stamps. I remember eating the government cheese, the kind that came in huge blocks. Our diet wasn't the best, which might explain some of my brain dysfunctions, but we did the best we could. In those days I cannot remember my parents ever watching the State of the Union address. I'm not sure the president's words would have made much difference to them.

I wonder if that's how the poor masses who heard Jesus as He spoke from the mountainside felt. His words were filled with hope and instruction, but could they really hear what He was saying?

Their plight was not unlike that of many poor people today. There was a rich elite that bought off the politicians. Many of the high-profile religious leaders of the time were spiritual prostitutes who gave spiritual cover to the misdeeds of politicians. Many of these people were broken on the shores of life, struggling for something worth believing in.

Enter Jesus.

"Blessed are the poor in spirit," the voice booms with a smile that

111

CAN YOU HEAR ME NOW?

could melt an iceberg, "for theirs is the kingdom of heaven." The promise was big and hairy like a Sasquatch and equally elusive.

They must have whispered to each other. "Did He just say what I think He said?"

"Yeah, girl, He did. I heard it with these two ears right here."

These words were radical, because heretofore heaven and the spoils therein were reserved for the learned, the elite, the perfectly coiffed, those with old money. "Not so!" yelled Jesus. This great place called heaven is reserved for the broken-spirited, meek-hearted, sobbing ones who have no one to champion their cause. Jesus cared.

The state of the union in Jesus' day wasn't much more sorry than it is today, but on that day the weaklings of society saw heaven, and for the first time it was theirs.

THE 411. . . . .

Read Jesus' sermon on the mount in its entirety (Matthew 5-7). Why didn't the people who heard Jesus' words regard them as empty pronouncements? What made Jesus believable?

God Gets a Laugh

"The wicked plot against the righteous and gnash their teeth at them; but the Lord laughs at the wicked" (Psalm 37:12, 13).

You really should hear my mother laugh. There's so much to love about Clarissa Jeannette Esmond. I love her food. I love her giving spirit. I love her counsel. But out of all those things, it is her laugh I love the most.

Hard times have silenced it somewhat, but oh, how I love to hear that laughter. The sound is high-pitched and deafening. The longer the joke, the louder her laugh becomes. It has been known to send my dad running from the room from time to time as he laments the sudden attack on his eardrums.

When Mama laughs, all is right with the world! For the moment there are no worries about bills or family problems. The sidesplitting karma she puts out is infectious. When she laughs, one cannot help joining in the experience.

When we think of what it means to laugh, we tend to think of it in purely human terms. Laughter is a God-given function that allows us to release tension, stress, and anxiety, not to mention the special healing chemicals that wash over the brain and help us feel better. But while God is the being who dreamed up the first laugh track, most of us probably struggle

112

Weird Godspeak

to think of Him as busting a gut while watching an episode of *Bernie Mac* or a *Seinfeld* rerun. Somehow that image doesn't seem to fit God, and I'm not sure I'd want the Master of the universe taking a break to watch *Seinfeld*. What about you?

In addition, I'm also not comfortable with the idea that the God I know and love is cackling loudly at the misfortune of human beings, even if those beings are wicked. That doesn't seem like a cool thing for God to do. Shouldn't God be feeling pain about those who go astray? Shouldn't He be pensive and thoughtful, serious and drawn? Nope, says the psalmist David. God laughs at the wicked and their plottings.

Before you start scratching your head, it may do some good for us to understand that David is the one doing the talking here. Yes, he is inspired by God to write what he is writing, but we must remember that the language David uses is not necessarily inspired; David's thoughts are inspired. The words might very well be his own, and not God's.

David's point is really a simple one: God's laughter is one of contempt for the deeds of the wicked. We puny mortals plot and scheme, as if the world is one big captainless ship out to sea. God sees us when we plan our dastardly deeds. He watches us when we do the dirty in secret. Nothing escapes His gaze. In fact, He doesn't just see us at the time we are working our game; He fast-forwards the DVD of our life and watches with sadness the closing scenes of our existence if we do not change.

The view from there is enough to make God chuckle. If God does laugh, rest assured that He is not amused, for His heart always beats for the sinner. It is tuned to the frequency of every human on Planet Earth, even the stupid ones who dare to live outside of His love.

THE 411. . . . .

The thirty-seventh psalm is truly amazing. If you have ever lost sleep over the plottings of the wicked, if you've ever wanted to slap the paint off someone who did you wrong, if you've ever dreamed of throwing Osama bin Laden into a tank filled with hungry sharks, if you've ever relished the thought of pulling out your boss's toenails one by one, this is the psalm for you. Enjoy—and by the way, calm down. Don't have a cow! Pray!

A New Thing

"Forget the former things; do not dwell on the past. See, I am doing a new thing! Now it springs up; do you not perceive it?" (Isaiah 43:18, 19).

It's Sabbath afternoon. A few friends have gathered at my home for lunch and a little face time. Tim and LaVerda are here. I love this couple. They are special people to me. Adia, the African princess, is here. She is a beautiful girl with a great sense of style and a heart for the Lord. She is cool. Chris and Kim are here with their beautiful children. A more God-fearing family you'll never find. Maurits and Cathy are also here, too. So are their lovely girls.

The joy of my life is also here—my girlfriend and wife, Kemba. She looks resplendent in a mind-altering red dress. She hugs me gently and steals secret smiles as we prepare lunch for the crew. *Oooh, I love this woman,* I muse to myself.

After lunch the women usually separate from us menfolk to do what women do. (Soon as I find out what that is, I'll let you know.) They are not missed too terribly, for by default I have the opportunity to steal a moment with my boy Tim. We love to talk about the Word of God.

Tim has taken to the Bible like a duck to water. He loves it. It consumes his life. He has learned to live out of the mouth of God, to hone in to the unmistakable, unshakable, imperishable voice of the Great One. In this way he is my mentor. His love for God's Word and the writings of the great author Ellen G. White is positively infectious. You cannot be around Timothy Golden without hearing a word from the Lord.

Today we have decided to wander around several passages. We turn the corner where Enoch is walking with God. We are moved by the idea that God would scoop up a human being because He wanted more face time with him. God loved to be with Enoch. We almost lost our minds as we read: "By faith Enoch was translated that he should not see death; and was not found, because God had translated him: for before his translation he had this testimony, that he pleased God" (Hebrews 11:5, KJV).

Can you say "sweet"? Imagine what it would be like to know that your life pleased God. I'm getting amped-up just thinking about it.

We continued walking through the Word until we came to the place where a teenage boy was being given his marching orders. "Before I formed you in the womb I knew you, before you were born I set you apart; I appointed you as a prophet to the nations" (Jeremiah 1:5).

Wow! God had set young Jerry aside long before he had breath. When

Weird Godspeak

the teen protested that he was but a child who didn't even know how to speak, God touched his mouth and placed His words in it (verse 9). Praise God! We were into full praise mode after reading this scripture.

Those passages were awesome, but the next one we came to was the big kahuna. This scripture nearly gave us an aneurysm. In Isaiah 43 God is wooing His wayward people back to Himself. Israel has sinned against God, joined themselves to idols, and prostituted themselves with other nations. Needless to say, God is not pleased.

Sprinkled throughout the book of Isaiah are dire warnings and predictions of God's imminent retribution. But in chapter 43 God opens a window of hope for His people. Isn't that just like God? He tells them, "Let's forget the past. I know you did many things to hurt Me. I know you failed Me, but let's move on. Let's try something new."

God goes on to talk about this new thing. He promises to vanquish the Babylonians, who are oppressing the Israelites. He promises them peace and safety, "a way in the desert and streams in the wasteland" (verse 19). In a sense God is making His final plea for Israel to change and return to Him.

By this point in our Bible study, Tim and I are filled up. We are speechless. We wonder silently, *What kind of God says, "The past is gone. Forget about it. I want to try something new, something that you've never experienced before. Let's try grace!"*

You serve an awesome God, friend. He lives to do new things. He is not bound by what you did in the past. He is not scared off by what you will do in the future. He is committed to seeing you walk with Him as Enoch did.

Wouldn't that be something new?

THE 411. . . . .
Read Isaiah 43 today. In many ways Israel did not accept God's offer of fresh grace. In what ways do you miss out on the new things God wishes to do for you? Why not carve out some time today to write a letter of repentance and change? The new can come only when the old is gone.

And God Said Yes!

"O sun, stand still over Gibeon, O moon, over the Valley of Aijalon" (Joshua 10:12).

Ever ask God for something big? I'm not talking about one of those halfhearted requests that you really don't believe you will receive. I'm talk-

115

CAN YOU HEAR ME NOW?

ing about something really, really huge, like say, the right person to marry or a free brand-new car when you know you have no money. Ever ask God for something really humongous?

What was His answer? Do you remember? Did you wait for Him to give it to you, or did you run off in a tizzy because His answer didn't fit your timetable, or worse—He didn't answer at all?

One point of clarification before we go any further: GOD ALWAYS ANSWERS. That's right. You might not want to hear that, but it really is true. GOD ALWAYS ANSWERS. Charles Cammack, an elder at my church, puts it this way: "There are three answers that God gives: Yes, Not yet, and I have something better for you." God never says NO. His no is as much a blessing as is His yes. That'll take a while to digest. It certainly took me a while to learn that lesson.

Now, back to the issue of asking God for big things. I would say that the largest request I've ever made of God was for Him to show me what my purpose is in life. I asked God to lead me into the profession that would bring Him the most glory. Who would have ever thought that He'd place me, a small Black kid with a temper the size of Mount Everest, in a position to lead others to Christ? I continue to be amazed at God's sense of humor.

A millimeter below this towering request was my desire to find the right person to spend my life with. Incidentally, I asked God for both of these things in the summer between graduating from high school and beginning college. This was crunch time for me. I felt the need to get serious about my life, and I approached my college years that way.

The answer to the first prayer kind of evolved. I was fairly good at English, so I kind of just decided to hide out as an English major until my real calling came along. Fat chance. My real calling was there all along, but I dreamed of bigger things, none of which I thought could be achieved by teaching English for the rest of my life. Boy, was I off the mark.

The answer to the next dilemma in my life is what I like to call "the sweetest, most luscious, most beautiful answered prayer ever." That's a mouthful to say, because my wife is quite a woman. God exceeded my wildest dreams a billion times over. I love my wife, but I don't deserve her.

Big audacious requests are nothing new to God. He's been honoring them from time immemorial. God answered Abraham and Sarah's prayer for a son when they were in rocking chairs. He elevated young Joseph to the height of political success from the depths of a pit. He's answered prayers from fiery furnaces, lions' dens, tumultuous seas, and a whole host of other places. God ain't scared of big petitions.

Weird Godspeak

That's what Joshua knew about God as the Israelites faced off against the Amorites. As the tide of the battle turned in Israel's favor, Joshua perceived that they would run out of day before they would be able to finish off the Amorites. So he did what any of us would do in the same situation, right? He asked God to freeze the day where it was. Isn't that what you do when you're trying to make a deadline or finish a big project?

I wonder what the Amorites were thinking at the time. *If we keep running, the day will soon be over, and we'll live to fight another day.* Wrong! As they peered to the heavens they noticed that the sun refused to move out of its place. Hour after hour, for 24 hours, the sun refused to move.

In the heat of battle Joshua made an insane request of God, and God said yes. He put the world on pause.

Why would God do such a thing? Well, I have the distinct feeling that Joshua's request lined up with God's will. That usually happens when one spends quality time finding out what God's will is through prayer, Bible study, and sharing one's faith. Second, I believe that the victory Joshua craved was aimed at bringing about God's glory. He didn't want God to stop the sun just so he could show off his connection with the Almighty. This victory would send a message to evil nations all around that Israel's God was "the" God, and they had better not mess with Him or His people.

You still might not want to ask God for something big, fearing that it will never materialize. I can hear God now: "Go ahead. Make My day!"

THE 411 . . . .

What has been your biggest answered prayer? Do you remember? Whom have you told about it? Tell someone what great things God has done for you—today.

Baby Killer?

"The Lord has taken away your sin. You are not going to die" (2 Samuel 12:13).

Whew! a visibly shaken king thought. *At least God isn't so angry with me that He would take my life. I know that I deserve to die for what I've done, but God has given me one more chance.*

That's got to be what David was thinking as he listened to the prophet Nathan's message from the Lord. You remember the story, don't you?

Can You Hear Me Now?

David sleeps with a soldier's wife while he is in battle, gets her pregnant, and tries to hide it by having the soldier murdered on the battlefield. Amazingly, the plan succeeds.

The Ammonites brutally kill Uriah, the Hittite, after King David arranges for him to be placed where the fighting is most fierce (2 Samuel 11:14, 15). King David, undaunted by the news of his servant's death, informs Bathsheba of the death of her husband, waits for the end of her period of mourning, and then makes her his wife. It's a story that no one in Hollywood could ever dream up.

For days David must have felt as though all was well between God and him. *Sure, there are whispers here and there, but no one can definitively prove anything,* he must have surmised. *I'm not that baby's daddy,* he must have told himself a million times. But no matter how hard he tried, he just couldn't shake the nagging sense that God was on his trail.

When the prophet Nathan unpacked David's sin, he was visibly shaken and rattled. He was cut to the heart. He felt the import, the weight, of what he had done, and he was sincerely sorrowful. He was repentant. He was not seeking simply to escape punishment. He knew he was wrong. Surely God would relent and have mercy, right?

Let's see if God does relent: "You killed him with the sword of the Ammonites. Now, therefore, the sword will never depart from your house, because you despised me and took the wife of Uriah the Hittite to be your wife. . . .

"Out of your own household I am going to bring calamity upon you. Before your very eyes I will take your wives and give them to one who is close to you, and he will lie with your wives in broad daylight. You did it in secret, but I will do this thing in broad daylight before all Israel" (2 Samuel 12:9-12).

Now, shouldn't God stop here? Surely the sight of someone close to David making love to his wives in broad daylight was punishment enough. Alas, it is not. God is not quite done yet. The bitter grape on which David will suck for the rest of his natural life gets even more revolting.

As David collapses under the weight of God's judgment, Nathan continues: "The Lord has taken away your sin. You are not going to die," he begins. "But because by doing this you have made the enemies of the Lord show utter contempt, the son born to you will die" (verses 13, 15).

Nathan had scarcely left the palace when God struck Bathsheba and David's "love" child.

I have often wondered, *Why did God kill David's child?* Was this really

Weird Godspeak

necessary? Didn't God make His point emphatically when He noted that the sword, or death, would never depart from David's house? Why did this innocent child have to perish?

I don't know if this is the right answer, but a friend of mine often makes a statement that I have found to be extremely profound: "The tragedy of sin is that someone innocent of all wrong has to pay for the sins of those who are guilty of wrong." The truth of this statement is borne out by the fact that Jesus endured a crucifixion for crimes He did not commit. He was the ultimate victim, taking on Himself the sins of the world. In a certain sense David and Bathsheba's offspring was a type of Christ, a kind of sacrificial lamb, paying for sins that the child never committed.

That answer works, but when I get to heaven, God has got some explaining to do. I want to know why!

THE 411. . . . .
Read the rest of this amazing episode in 2 Samuel 12. How did God show that David was forgiven? What does that tell you about God?

Don't Worry, Be Happy?

"Therefore do not worry about tomorrow, for tomorrow will worry about itself" (Matthew 6:34).

Terrorism.

Wars.

Famines.

Disasters by land, sea, and air.

Divorce.

HIV and AIDS.

Weak economy.

Unemployment.

Murder.

Greed.

Depravity.

Infanticide.

Matricide.

Patricide.

Suicide.

Trouble.

Can You Hear Me Now?

Immorality.

Sin.

God says that we should not worry. How is that possible in our world? Has God lost it? In a word—No! Here's what He means: "Therefore I tell you, do not worry about your life, what you will eat or drink; or about your body, what you will wear. Is not life more important than food, and the body more important than clothes?

"Look at the birds of the air; they do not sow or reap or store away in barns, and yet your heavenly Father feeds them. Are you not much more valuable than they? Who of you by worrying can add a single hour to his life?

"And why do you worry about clothes? See how the lilies of the field grow. They do not labor or spin. Yet I tell you that not even Solomon in all his splendor was dressed like one of these. If that is how God clothes the grass of the field, which is here today and tomorrow is thrown into the fire, will he not much more clothe you, O you of little faith?

"So do not worry, saying, 'What shall we eat?' or 'What shall we drink?' or 'What shall we wear?' For the pagans run after all these things, and your heavenly Father knows that you need them. But seek first his kingdom and his righteousness, and all these things will be given to you as well. Therefore do not worry about tomorrow, for tomorrow will worry about itself. Each day has enough trouble of its own" (Matthew 6:25-34).

THE 411. . . . .

There was a reason Jesus tried to turn the attention of His hearers to the things of nature. Noted spiritual commentator Ellen G. White writes this: "Christ sought to draw the attention of His disciples away from the artificial to the natural. . . . Why did not our heavenly Father carpet the earth with brown or gray? He chose the color that was most restful, the most acceptable to the senses" (*Review and Herald,* Oct. 27, 1885).

A God who would put that much thought into the color of grass is capable of handling anything we throw at Him. Cast all your cares upon Him!

CHAPTER 9

Where God Speaks

Off-limits

"And pray in the Spirit on all occasions with all kinds of prayers and requests. With this in mind, be alert and always keep on praying for all the saints" *(Ephesians 6:18).*

Have you ever felt a little self-conscious about praying in public? Such as when your plane is sitting on the runway ready for takeoff or just before you eat at a favorite restaurant? Perhaps you are one of those fearless people with nerves of steel who don't mind praying in public, or maybe you whisper one of those internal prayers that run through the mind and bear no outward expression. I'll bet that's what you do.

I must admit: I get a little antsy about public displays of reflection toward God. I'm not sure why that is, but it sure doesn't stop God from impressing me to pray for people in some of the strangest places.

One time a delivery guy came to my home, quite late, to deliver a mattress. My cup of anger had basically run over by the time he arrived. It took all of my strength not to "bless" this guy.

I looked to see if he had a partner with him. He didn't, which meant that I would have to help him bring in the mattress. We fought hard to get it up to the third-floor bedroom where my wife—who else—wanted it to go. As he prepared to leave, we started talking.

He told me about his family, his past jobs, and the fact that his delivery partner was very sick. He had made all the deliveries that day by himself—and we were the last ones.

Before I knew it, a familiar voice began whispering something to me.

121

CAN YOU HEAR ME NOW?

"You should pray with this man, Dwain," the voice said. "Encourage him. Don't let him leave before you pray with him."

I wasn't sure how to respond. As I thought about it, the usual excuses bubbled up to the surface. *It's been a long day for this guy, Dwain; why keep him any longer? Are you going to pray right here in the foyer of your home? The door is wide open; your neighbors can probably see you. You can pray for this guy after he leaves.*

I refused to listen to the excuses.

"James"—he had introduced himself earlier—"do you mind if I say a prayer for you?"

"No," he replied warmly. "I don't mind at all. Let's pray."

I bowed my head and began praying for James right there in my foyer. After we finished, he thanked me profusely, so much so that I was really overwhelmed. To me it was really a simple gesture, nothing to write home about, but to him it was much more. Later that night I thanked God for giving me the right words to say and for sending His Holy Spirit to speak to me.

Long before the experience with James, I have felt the need to pray with people at the time when they share a burden or problem with me. When one of my neighbors lost his father, he saw me mowing my lawn, and he came over. With tears in his eyes he told me how much he loved his father, how much he missed him. Almost before he could get the words out, the same voice prompted me again: "Pray with Dean, Dwain. He needs to hear a prayer to Me."

I simply couldn't let that moment slip away—rather, God wouldn't let that moment slip away. I could hear His voice urging me to pray for my friend right there on the front lawn. When we finished, he seemed to feel better.

Through the years I've learned that there's really no place that's off limits to God's voice. I think God looks at the situations people face in life, sizes them up, and reaches for His nearest operative. He sends us a clear message of what He wants done—perhaps a prayer, a offer of help, a kind word, a warm hug. If we are open to His voice and willing to act on what we hear, God will continue to fill our ears with His voice. And the more we listen and obey, the clearer it gets.

THE 411. . . . .

Read Matthew 6:1-14. Does Jesus condemn all public acts of righteousness? What problem was Jesus seeking to address?

Where God Speaks

During His ministry Jesus healed, prayed, and shared His faith in public. What was different about His ministry as opposed to that of the Pharisees?

Perfect Timing

"For he will deliver the needy who cry out, the afflicted who have no one to help" (Psalm 72:12).

As I prepared to speak that Sabbath, I got a little queasy. Actually, I was fine until I was introduced as the speaker for the morning. That's when the butterflies (or should I say buzz saws) started shredding my innards.

You shouldn't be scared, I comforted myself. *You've done this before. You've "preached" in prisons, hospitals, churches, homes; what's so different about this time?* The words cycled through my brain like a bunch of BMX racers, but they made no tracks. No matter how much I tried to self-medicate my fear, I was still unsettled.

This was hardly the best way to launch my "reign" as editor of *Insight* magazine. What would this church think when my sermon flopped? I imagined word of my lame sermon flying around the country, poisoning all future invitations.

I had arrived earlier the day before and couldn't help feeling that this was going to be a great engagement. The warm Miami breezes transformed a cold Philadelphia November into the most tropical of paradises. The young woman who had asked me to be the speaker for the youth day program was a good friend from college. The pastor of the church was the father of another good friend. This should be a walk in the park, right? Wrong.

It didn't help things much that the service was great. The youth choir was "slammin'," led by a young woman who sounded ready for a record deal. The church was applauding each song, and the anticipation in the air was palpable. You could taste it.

All of which only served to deepen my sense of despair. *Jesus Himself couldn't live up to this hype,* I thought. *What's more, I'm not even a "real" preacher. I have no degrees in theology.* The negative self-talk was getting the best of me as the choir began the song of meditation, the one right before the sermon.

Quietly I wished that the song would never end. As I listened prayerfully, I reached out to God. I said to Him, with all the faith I could muster, *I trust You, Lord. You will have to make Yourself visible so that everyone here can see You. Please be with me.*

123

CAN YOU HEAR ME NOW?

Just then God brought back to my mind something that Pastor Byrd had said to me. As we sat in his study preparing for the service, he told me what a blessing it was to have me there. He encouraged me more than he knew.

Before we left for the pulpit he said, "Dwain, you are no different than any of the great preachers in our church."

What? I thought to myself. *Is he serious? Can I really be compared to the Barry Blacks, Mark Finleys, Walter Pearsons, etc.?* He couldn't be serious. I waited to hear what he would say next, since that statement was obviously a joke.

But he wasn't joking. "Dwain, you have the same message they have." His statement instantly reminded me of something another wise mentor once told me, "We don't have great preachers; we have a great message."

As the choir ended their song, I felt peace descend on me like a dove. God had spoken to me at just the right time. I couldn't have planned it better.

THE 411. . . . .
Read Acts 1. What were the disciples waiting for? What happened when they got it? Where do we get the power to serve God? Do some people have more of the Holy Spirit than others?

The Big One
"He said to me, 'Son of man, stand up on your feet and I will speak to you'" *(Ezekiel 2:1).*

It's like getting a call from your boss for a little private one-on-one; or like your parents summoning you for a teachable moment—not exactly something you look forward to. In everybody's life there are defining moments, make-or-break moments, pressure-packed moments.

For instance, when you forget the day you and your girlfriend began "going steady," you're treading on the borders of annihilation. When that same girlfriend becomes your wife and continues to recall every obscure significant date as though it happened yesterday, you remember not to forget. If you do, there's a day of reckoning coming, a time of great tribulation when the couch becomes your temporary residence and refuge. You understand that this is pure conjecture. I've never experienced anything like that.

When my wife gets upset over something, she gets calm. I dread hav-

124

Where God Speaks

ing to talk to her. I almost wish she would explode. Then I could use her outburst to feign a mortal injury, thereby seizing the high ground. Ah, but it never works out that way.

She doesn't get belligerent or bellicose. No shouting accompanies her anger. No "cussin'" ensues. No skillets or frying pans go whizzing by. She just gets quiet, and a pained look of disgust covers her beautiful face like a storm cloud. Trust me, it's one of the few things I fear.

No matter what I think of myself, at moments like these I sense the end of myself, for my wife knows me and lives with my mess.

I believe that's how Ezekiel felt that day by the Kebar River when God took time out from running the universe to pay him a visit. Imagine the president of the United States of America pulling up in front of your house, complete with a retinue of security service personnel, helicopters buzzing overhead, and CNN carrying shots of your home live.

Ezekiel had just made the big-time. This moment would forever define his life. God was knocking at his door, and he couldn't really say, "Come back tomorrow."

It's one thing to worship God in a synagogue; it's another thing to see Him face to face. It's one thing to read the Bible; it's quite another to see the Bible come alive in front of you. That's what happens when God visits you, when God comes for a little one-on-one.

Ezekiel, a Babylonian captive at the time, was probably down by the river taking a swim, or perhaps he was washing his clothes or lamenting about the degradation and embarrassment of living as slaves in a foreign land. As the son of a priest, he keenly felt the humiliation, because he no doubt knew that God was the one who ultimately allowed it to happen.

The blue sky turned ominous as the clouds recoiled at the presence of the Almighty. As Ezekiel beheld the scene he saw strange wheellike beasts. Ezekiel then saw God. "I saw that from what appeared to be his waist up he looked like glowing metal, as if full of fire, and that from there down he looked like fire; and brilliant light surrounded him. Like the appearance of a rainbow in the clouds on a rainy day, so was the radiance around him" (Ezekiel 1:27, 28).

When Ezekiel saw God, he immediately fell on his face. Then God spoke to him. Ezekiel was called to prophesy the destruction of Jerusalem, God's judgment on Israel and the surrounding nations, and how God would restore His glory to the people He loved more than anything else in the world.

Most of us read such a scripture and conclude that God no longer

CAN YOU HEAR ME NOW?

scrolls back the heavens to speak to us. "A thing of the past," we decide. I beg to differ with you. Wherever we are, whether in school, at work, walking through the countryside or the downtown of some major city, God can and will open the heavens to speak to us. We need not be afraid. We need only to be ready.

THE 411. . . . .

Read Ezekiel 1. Do you think there were others around who saw what Ezekiel saw? When God speaks to us, does He leave others out of the conversation?

When You Pray

"Put your hope in God, for I will yet praise him, my Savior and my God" (Psalm 42:11).

It had all the makings of a great day. I got up that morning at 5:45. I lay there for a while to see if the clock was playing some cruel trick on me, since it seemed like only five minutes ago that I had fallen asleep. Alas, the clock was truthful—as usual. It was time to get cracking.

I wiped the sleep from my eyes and stretched as I rolled over to grab my Bible—one of the good habits I'm trying to make stick. After my worship it was time for a quick shower, a word of prayer by phone with my wife in Philadelphia, and off to work.

I like to get to work by 7:00 a.m. That's the time I usually do my power walk. On this brisk November day the 35-degree temperature dared me to challenge its frigid blast. I was undaunted. I got out and started hiking around the building. Soon I was warm enough to start belting out a few tunes. (I highly recommend singing in the cold—don't knock it till you try it.)

I launched into a song I first fell in love with in high school: " 'When you pray, everything will be all right.' " The artist was a guy named Chris Willis. Right now I wish there were a way to add music to these words. I really can't explain his sound. He is a unique talent, created to glorify God.

The song continues: "If you stay, everything will work out fine. Just have faith/when you pray/When you need a friend/When you need a friend/just have faith when you pray." The more I sang, the faster I walked. The faster I walked, the louder I sang. I was in the middle of a major praise session. I felt as though God had sent a skid of angels to sing

Where God Speaks

with me. Of course, I'm not sure what my coworkers thought as they heard what was coming from my mouth.

It was slightly an hour later when I got a call from my wife as she left home for work. "Hi, hon," she started, "how are you?"

Still buzzing from my amazing walk, I quickly answered. "Pretty good. What's up?"

Her voice got softer as she gave me the news. "Well, sweetheart, I went outside to head to work, and I noticed that Winston Foster was missing."

We name our cars. This one we bought from a husband and wife—the wife's maiden name was Winston and their last name was Foster. Go figure.

My wife never raised her voice, never got frantic or out of sorts. This is vintage Kemba. She's a fairly calm person in times of crisis. Her storms rage within, while mine tend to blow up on the outside for the world to see.

I felt my stomach do a strange little wiggle as I processed the news. I wasn't sure how to react, but I wasn't about to lose it on the phone with my wife. Just a week earlier her brother had been in a terrible accident, and the last thing she needed was a "priest" who couldn't lead the family to the source of comfort and hope.

"OK," I managed. "It's possible that the car was towed, or it might have been stolen. Let's pray." We prayed together about the situation and said goodbye. This was my chance to find out the meaning of the words I had sung so loudly a few hours earlier. Satan had designed a test aimed right at my praise. As I sank back in my chair, I could see the clouds of doubt begin to gather around me.

That's when I heard a voice encouraging me to open the Bible to Psalm 42. For a moment I hesitated. *This is stupid,* I thought. *God doesn't work this way. He's a God of order. Maybe you should look in the concordance for some encouragement and go from there.* However, I decided to obey the voice, and I was glad I did.

I read the entire psalm in search of that special "Godword." It came in verse 5, then again in the final verse, 11. King David is feeling a little depressed for whatever reason. In his despair he questions his discouragement and closes with this triumphant refrain, not once but twice: "Put your hope in God, for I will yet praise him, my Savior and my God."

That day God found me on the way to a place I knew very well. Just as I prepared to enter a dark sanctuary of doubt and questioning, He barred the door with a promise written across the entrance: "Put your hope in God" (verse 11). I thanked Him and began the search for an old

CAN YOU HEAR ME NOW?

wayward BMW. Tune in tomorrow for the second episode of this Winston Foster caper.

THE 411. . . . .
Get a piece of paper and a pencil. Are you ready? Think of the last big crisis in your life. Write it down. Don't leave out any details. Write down the moment when you knew that things were going to work out. Was it before or after the circumstances changed?

Everything Will Be All Right

"Therefore I tell you, whatever you ask for in prayer, believe that you have received it, and it will be yours" (Mark 11:24).

Now that I knew God was with me, it was time to find my favorite ride. My car is not what you would call a showpiece. In fact, it's more piece than show.

It first rolled off a Bavarian Motor Works assembly line in 1984. Back then it was quite a car. One hundred eighty-five horses pulled along a stunning package of power everything, leather everything, not to mention that killer inline 6 engine. In 1984 my BMW 633 CSi could run with the best of them.

But that was then, and this is now. My car is several years removed from its prime. It doesn't have any 2005 gadgetry in it, but there's something timeless about my "shark" (that's BMW-speak for the 6 series). It's considered a classic, since BMW stopped making the 6 series in 1989.

Fully restored, my car would fetch some nice coin, but not in its present condition. The speedometer and odometer don't work. The spoiler on the front end is broken. When I shift gears, a loud whiny sound alerts everyone within earshot that a dinosaur just passed gas. It's not cute, but it's mine, and I dreamed that one day I would fix up my shark. I think all men come with a chip and a warning that says, "WHEN ACTIVATED, MALE MAY SPEND MEANINGLESS HOURS AND MONEY ON OLD OBSOLETE VEHICLE. SHOULD THESE SIGNS OCCUR, REMOVE CHIP IMMEDIATELY."

I started the hunt by calling my friend, attorney Timothy Golden, a Philadelphia insider if there ever was one.

"Tim-dog"—that's friend for the ebonically challenged—"what's goin' on?"

Where God Speaks

"Hey, Dwain, what's hapnin', man?" he snorted.

"I'm good, Tim. Look, dude, I got a little problem, and I was wondering if you could give me some advice."

"Yeah, Dwain," he answered, "whatever you need, man." I must say here that Tim Golden is one of the most helpful and generous people I know. If he can do something for someone, consider it done. This is a friend who goes shopping and brings me back shirts, ties, and cuff link sets. If you don't have a Tim in your life, I feel sorry for you. But this one is taken.

"Tim, I think my car was either towed or stolen last night. Any idea where I should begin looking for it?" Like clockwork Tim had the answer.

"Sure, Dwain. I'm sorry about your car, man. I'll be praying for you and Kemba that God will work everything out." That's the other thing I love about Timothy Golden. He prays for me.

"Here's what you do, Dwain. Call the Philadelphia Parking Authority. Start there. If the city towed it, they would know where to look." I thanked Tim and started to call around.

Tim was right. The parking authority did not have a record of my car, but they led me to the office where abandoned vehicles are processed, which led me to Lou's Towing Service, which led me to Winston Foster.

A few days earlier I had removed my license plates to have them changed, and some well-meaning person had called the abandoned vehicles office. I guess they took one look at my "hoopty" with no tags and decided it was a blight on the neighborhood. To get my car I would have to pay towing and storage fees, and I'd be on the road again.

Where does God speak? I am witness that God speaks comfort and peace in the middle of trials and heartaches. When you get flustered, take note of your surroundings. That's the place you will praise God.

The 411...

Think about the following statement. After reading it, thank God for working out your challenges and ask God to help you to trust Him more.

"We are not to let the future, with its hard problems, its unsatisfying prospects, make our hearts faint, our knees tremble, our hands hang down. . . . Those who surrender their lives to His guidance and to His service will never be placed in a position for which He has not made provision" (Ellen G. White, *The Ministry of Healing,* p. 248).

Video Store

"Where can I go from your Spirit? Where can I flee from your presence?"
(Psalm 139:7).

In my heart I knew I shouldn't have gone there. I knew better. What's more, God tried to tell me not to go, but I didn't listen.

Every city has one of them. They are usually on the outskirts of town in rural communities or relegated to the "red light district" in major cities. They're open 24 hours a day, and the cast of characters hiding in the shadows going in and out at all hours of the day or night range from businessmen to homosexuals and everyone in between.

Growing up, I remember going into video stores before there was Blockbuster and other video chains that cater to families. The video stores in my neighborhood had the family videos in the front of the store and the real moneymakers in the back.

Usually there'd be a door with a sign that read "Must Be 18 or Older to Enter." That was enough to scare me off. At the time I wasn't 18, and I sure wasn't going to sneak in there and get caught by the manager. But I was curious.

What's behind that door? I often wondered. From time to time you'd see some older guy sneak in there when he thought no one was looking. However, there were others who were bold. They just marched in, and it didn't much matter if there were women or children around. That was the other thing that scared me off.

But the time came when I decided I wanted to take a look for myself. I was old enough. I even had a driver's license. I wasn't ever going to rent one of those videos. I wasn't bold enough to take it up to the counter and look some woman in the face as I walked out with *Debbie Does Dallas.* I just couldn't picture me doing that.

I walked into the store, looked around for a while, and started for the private door in the back. At the time I felt as if that door were separating me from some higher experience that I just had to have. I had to satisfy my curiosity. Just one look, and I would never go back in there again.

I went in, and almost immediately my heart started pounding, racing. The walls were covered with movie boxes whose titles and pictures I dare not mention. As my eyes beheld the scene, I could hear God speak to me in a clear refrain. *You don't belong here, Dwain. Why don't you leave now? This is not for you. I am with you, and you cannot stay here.*

I heard God, but I resisted His voice. I really didn't want to hear Him

Where God Speaks

at that moment. Like Adam and Eve, I longed to know good and evil, to see what was behind the door. As I walked in farther I could see the other "Johns," many of whom looked like "porno pros." I could tell by the way they scrupulously examined each video. They had been there often. At the sight of them I decided it was time to go.

As you might imagine, I struggled about sharing that story with you. Most of us, if we're honest, don't relish the thought of showing people our warts. I certainly don't. I would much rather tell you about what a great person I am, but that's only part of the story. The rest of the story is the regret I am forced to live with because of poor decisions.

That day in the video store I opened up a vein in my spiritual life and invited Satan to fill it with poison. He did. But I am encouraged and thankful for the assurance of God's forgiveness and the realization that no matter where I go, God's Spirit is with me, leading me in the path of right-doing—righteousness.

Does God free me to do whatever, to keep going to forbidden places? No. But when we fall, when we fail God, He doesn't throw us away. He tells us to rise up and walk.

I cannot change the decision I made that day, or its consequences, but I can submit my will to God today. I think I'm going to do that right now.

THE 411. . . . .

Read 1 John 1:9. What sin are you really struggling to overcome? Have you asked God to forgive you? Do you believe that you are forgiven and that He will help you overcome? Don't give up on yourself. God hasn't given up on you!

Reluctant Warrior

"When the Israelites cried to the Lord because of Midian, he sent them a prophet, who said, 'This is what the Lord, the God of Israel, says'" (Judges 6:7, 8).

It's Thanksgiving, and you can't wait to get home to feast at your mother's table. I won't bother to tempt you with a list of the usual Thanksgiving delicacies—tender turkey glazed with a dollop of honey, stuffing so soft it floats, baked chicken, apple pie, sweet potato pie—since I'm a recovering vegetarian. You get my drift, right? If I wrote any more about my former Thanksgiving favorites, I'd probably have a major relapse. It has happened before.

131

Can You Hear Me Now?

As you walk in the door, tantalizing smells greet your nostrils; you start to drool. Your folks welcome you home and sit you in the favorite spot at the table. Your mom grabs your plate and loads it down with everything in sight. Then she puts the plate in front of you and urges you to eat. By now you are drooling all over the plate. (It's fair to say that no one would dare grab anything off your plate, having seen the river in your mouth overflow its banks.)

You grab the knife, scoop up the fork with reckless abandon, and dive into the meal, when something startles you and everyone else. The front door of the house swings open. Your family may have been expecting guests, but these people are no guests of yours.

They are a hated gang of marauders who have been terrorizing small communities across the state. There's got to be at least 70 to 80 of them surrounding your house. They come in, knock you over, and proceed to eat everything in sight. Unfortunately, they don't leave when they are finished. Instead, they force your mom to cook more food, and they devour that. They stay for what seems like forever, until nothing is left.

Now imagine if they came back every year around the same time and there was nothing you could do about it. You'd get a little fed up, right?

That, in a nutshell, is how Israel felt each year during the harvesting season. Because of Israel's idolatry, God allowed the Midianites to conquer them. The Midianites exploited the Israelites, taking everything they had. Each year during the harvest season, usually a time of celebration and thanksgiving, the Midianites, Amalekites, and other Eastern peoples would invade the country like a swarm of locusts. They would squat on the land, eat everything in sight, and that which they could not eat, they would destroy. They left nothing for the Israelites.

Enter God. While Israel deserved what they got for abandoning "the" God for the gods of their oppressors, heaven heard their cries.

"When the Israelites cried to the Lord because of Midian, he sent them a prophet, who said, 'This is what the Lord, the God of Israel, says'" (Judges 6:7, 8). It was just what they needed to hear, but the prophet was a little reluctant.

"The angel of the Lord came and sat down under the oak in Ophrah that belonged to Joash the Abiezrite, where his son Gideon was threshing wheat in a winepress to keep it from the Midianites. When the angel of the Lord appeared to Gideon, he said, 'The Lord is with you, mighty warrior.'

"'But sir,' Gideon replied, 'if the Lord is with us, why has all this happened to us? Where are all his wonders that our fathers told us about when

132

Where God Speaks

they said, "Did not the Lord bring us up out of Egypt?" But now the Lord has abandoned us and put us into the hand of Midian.'

"The Lord turned to him and said, 'Go in the strength you have and save Israel out of Midian's hand. Am I not sending you?'

"'But Lord,' Gideon asked, 'how can I save Israel? My clan is the weakest in Manasseh, and I am the least in my family.'

"The Lord answered, 'I will be with you, and you will strike down all the Midianites together.'

"Gideon replied, 'If now I have found favor in your eyes, give me a sign that it is really you talking to me. Please do not go away until I come back and bring my offering and set it before you.'

"And the Lord said, 'I will wait until you return'" (verses 11-18).

Young Gideon went in and prepared an offering to God, and when he came back he was floored to see God waiting under the oak, right where he had left Him.

As we know, Gideon went on to destroy the altars to Baal that the Israelites had erected. He also defeated the massive armies of the Midianites with a skeleton crew of 300 men, so that there'd be no doubt who won the battle, you understand.

What I really like about Gideon's story is the gentle way that God dealt with him. He was a "country boy," not given to extravagance. He was fearful and timid, but God saw something special in Him, something worth the effort. So God arranged an audience with him at, of all places, a winepress.

Perhaps like Gideon, you're hiding out in some hidden corner of your life, some spot far away from prying eyes. Is God welcome there? Can He come there and commune with you?

THE 411. . . . .

This week we looked at some of the places where God speaks to us. Say a prayer, asking God to come into every part of your life. Leave no place off-limits. Give Him full control of everything. Pray this prayer every day for at least three weeks. Remember, each time you pray this prayer God will come, so mean what you say.

Then make some time to write down what happened, how you changed, and how God spoke to you.

CHAPTER 10

Verbal Assassins

No Love From the Street

"Isn't this the carpenter? Isn't this Mary's son and the brother of James, Joseph, Judas and Simon? Aren't his sisters here with us?" (Mark 6:3).

There is a tug-of-war that has been playing out in the sports world over the past few years. It has nothing to do with whether high-priced, overpaid athletes should get more money or who will win the NBA title or the Super Bowl. No, this struggle is much more understated, evident only to close observers.

No other athlete embodies the struggle more than Allen Iverson, the six-foot phenom who plays basketball for the Philadelphia 76ers. Iverson is a breathtaking talent if for no other reason than the fact that he is a midget in a land of giants. While officially listed at six feet in height, he is closer to 5'11".

He possesses an amazing cadre of skills. He can handle the rock like a point guard, dishing it with the best of them. He can score like a shooting guard, and his manic defense allows him to lead the league in steals each year.

A mere 165 pounds of pure heart, Iverson fearlessly attacks the basket with the ball, often bearing the brunt of countless hip checks and body blocks. He constantly plays through numerous injuries that would render mere mortals immobile. He is special.

But for all his prowess on the court, it is Iverson's actions off the court that garner him the most attention. He has had several scrapes with the law, from the bowling alley ruckus that landed him in prison to allegedly beating his wife and putting her out of the house naked. It must be noted

134

Verbal Assassins

here that in many cases Iverson has been exonerated of all charges.

However, one would assume that Iverson grows tired of being seen as a thug. When not on the court, he dons baggy shorts, oversized T-shirts, and all the "ice" he can find. The ensemble comes complete with cornrowed hair, a bevy of tattoos blanketing his skin, and that ever-present disdain.

Iverson's image is no Madison Avenue construct, however. No PR consultants have been able to bend his style to suit the taste of the masses, as they did Michael Jordan during his reign as king of the sport. Iverson is the anti-Jordan, the prophet for a new generation who cut their teeth on hip-hop and attitude. And they have made him a Wall Street icon.

Allen Iverson refuses to change because, as he has noted, this is who he was before he got famous. For him to change now would mean a loss of street creed. He would be looked upon as a sellout. To sell out would mean no love from the street, and the street means everything.

So instead of jettisoning his entourage of dawgs from the hood who seem to get him into trouble—for instance, the one who was smoking marijuana in his car—he sticks close to his roots. These are the people who believed in him, who nourished him, when no one else cared. When he returns home to his native Virginia, the folks in his neighborhood mob him. He put them on the map.

There is a certain charm to the Iverson story that reminds us of another superstar in the making. Rewind the tape 2,000 years or so. The Middle East is abuzz about a new phenom who heals people with a single word, preaches a gospel that is the envy of the religious establishment, and has a squeaky-clean image that everyone gravitates to. In a phrase, He's got "mad skillz."

One day the Phenom decided to go home to Nazareth, the place where He honed His skills and prepared for His ministry. But instead of a parade, the people who knew Him best—who remembered the boy who always was willing to help them in the fields, the one who would look out for the younger kids, the kid who could be trusted to deliver a message without broadcasting it to the world—were looking at Him out of the corner of their eyes.

He hadn't really changed, but the world was now acknowledging what they had known all along but had failed to accept: He was special. He was the Messiah.

The Bible says that when Jesus spoke in the synagogue that fateful Sabbath day, the neighbors marveled at His wisdom, but grew jealous of His claim to be the Messiah. So instead of celebrating Him, they "dissed" Him.

135

CAN YOU HEAR ME NOW?

Jesus came to bring a better life to the town that had been much maligned as a place for robbers, prostitutes, and crooked politicians. He came back home to heal the sick and suffering, to share God's love with everyone. But it was not to be.

John Mark writes, "He could not do any miracles there, except lay his hands on a few sick people and heal them. And he was amazed at their lack of faith" (Mark 6:5, 6).

The hometown crowd that witnessed the local Boy make it big couldn't help questioning His power, and with each question, with each doubt, they quenched the blessing in store for them.

When Jesus left Nazareth, a part of Him died.

THE 411. . . . .

Why did the people of Nazareth act the way they did toward Jesus? Why wasn't He welcomed?

Christian writer Ellen G. White comments: "They had seen Him toiling up and down the hills, they were acquainted with His brothers and sisters, and knew His life and labors. They had seen Him develop from childhood to youth, and from youth to manhood. Although His life had been spotless, they would not believe that He was the Promised One" (*The Desire of Ages*, p. 237).

A Little Humble Pie

"Here comes that dreamer!" (Genesis 37:19).

Dreams and dreamers are a dime a dozen. Doesn't everyone harbor some desire for greatness, some latent hankering to be the next "big" thing on the world stage?

A few years ago, before Wall Street scandals humbled corporate America, a very public dogfight was going on. Ted Turner, media mogul and corporate tycoon, engaged a bidding war with Microsoft founder Bill Gates. The two were not bidding on some piece of fine art valued at a price equal to that of a small country. No, they seemed to be waging war for the title of "Most Generous Corporate Raider."

Turner began making generous donations to educational institutions, global peace efforts, etc. But it was his gift to the United Nations that caught the attention of the world. The U.S. owed the United Nations more than $1 billion in dues. Turner evidently saw an opportunity to set-

Verbal Assassins

tle up with the U.N., so he gave them the single largest philanthropic gift ever given—$1 billion." "Take that, Bill Gates," he seemed to say.

In Gates's case, his generosity seemed to be perfectly timed to coincide with the huge antitrust lawsuit filed by the government against Microsoft for its monopolistic behavior. It also didn't hurt that he was taking a little ribbing from the aforementioned Turner, who made no secret of his contempt for Gates, the new king of the money hill. So Gates began giving away gobs of money, none of which he could possibly miss: $200 million here; $50 million there. Gates now captured the headlines and the good graces of the SEC.

I'm sure both Ted Turner and William Gates had noble intentions when they made their generous gifts. No one but God can really judge the motives of their hearts. That said, the timing of their gifts and the chatter surrounding them leads one to believe that theirs is a game of show-and-tell.

I've often wondered why CEOs who make their fortunes running over puny humans and mere mortals suddenly have an attack of conscience when they become "top dog." It seems that only then do they pause long enough to examine the world they have transcended. Not content to have conquered their sphere of business, they seek to be thought of as "good" people, and quite often they try to accomplish this by buying their way in.

Perhaps they also do it to buy the goodwill of their competitors, those whom they have vanquished along the way. In the case of Microsoft, several companies that were almost driven to extinction by Microsoft saw in the government's action an opportunity to kill the dreamer and his dreams. But they failed. A chastened Microsoft continues its dominance of all things PC.

The ancient Bible story of Joseph's betrayal at the hands of his brothers bears some resemblance to the tale of Gates and his competitors. Joseph was the favorite of his father, Jacob, the love child he sired with his favorite wife, Rachel.

Jacob also loved Joseph's half brothers, but they were the product of failed relationships. Although their mothers remained in Jacob's care, everyone knew whom he favored. The brothers were old enough to see the double standard. They would work all day and return to the camp sweaty, dusty, and weatherworn. Traipsing about in an audacious coat was a clean, perfectly coiffed Joseph. Even at the end of long, tiring days he would still eat before his brothers.

Thus the plot was hatched. The brothers spent their downtime in the fields obsessing about their privileged little brother. The situation got so bad that Reuben, the oldest, looked for opportunities to change the sub-

CAN YOU HEAR ME NOW?

ject. He knew Joseph was in danger, but he dared not take Joseph's side.

Just then Joseph approached, skipping along, singing, and wearing his coat of many colors. Every one of them wanted a piece of him. "Come now, let's kill him and throw him into one of these cisterns and say that a ferocious animal devoured him" (Genesis 37:20). The words cut through the air like a ninja sword. The brothers' verbal assault was more than pre-assassination banter. Were it not for a quick-thinking Reuben, Joseph would be dead.

Reuben thought as fast as he could. "'Let's not take his life,' he said. 'Don't shed any blood. Throw him into this cistern here in the desert, but don't lay a hand on him'" (verses 21, 22). As Joseph arrived, they stripped him and placed him in the cistern. A few hours later they sold him to the Ishmaelites.

Joseph's brothers should be blamed for the treacherous way they disposed of their little brother. But in Jacob's family there was plenty of blame to go around. A doting father created a volatile situation in his home. And Joseph, about 17 at the time, seemed to wave his special status in the face of his brothers, raising their ire. This seems to be borne out by the fact that they never plotted to kill Benjamin, the other son by Rachel.

When God singles us out for a holy purpose, He also gives a healthy dose of humility. It pays to be humble at all times, especially when the tough times come.

THE 411. . . . .

Read Genesis 37. How did Joseph's brothers seek to hide their crime? If you were a family counselor back in those days, how would you counsel this family? What would you say to Jacob?

The Real

"Son of man, prophesy against the prophets of Israel who are now prophesying" (Ezekiel 13:2).

I'll never forget the day in junior high school that I prepared for a big basketball game. I was on the seventh-grade team, and we were preparing to do battle against the eighth graders, who were favored to destroy us. But we were fearless.

Like any teenager, I asked my folks to hook me up with some "phat" kicks for the game. They took one look at me and ruled out the shoes I

138

Verbal Assassins

wanted. I dreamed of soaring through the air in some shell-toe Adidas sneakers. What I got instead was a knockoff brand that had half a shell-toe, four stripes, and no name.

"I can't wear these," I protested, but to no avail. Those were the ones my parents could afford, and they were not about to change their minds. They really didn't care about my rep as much as I did. I wonder why?

As the day of the game approached, I came up with a novel idea. *Maybe I could copy the Adidas logo onto my shoes.* It was another one of my brilliant schemes. The logo was in black, but since a blue pen was all I could find, I began the careful duplication of the Adidas logo. Each leaf was captured with the precision of a counterfeiter making $100 bills. The lettering was not perfect, but who would notice that when my feet would be moving at lightning speed.

But, I didn't count on one thing—heat.

I got to the game in time and laced up my fake Adidas sneakers. I made sure to avoid going over to the bleachers where the students were sitting. The last thing I needed was for someone to see my shoes and expose me.

The game soon began, and I was dashing around the court. We were doing pretty well, actually. The eighth graders could never put us away. Midway through the second half we were leading. Somehow I managed to glance at my sneakers, only to notice that the logo was smudged mercilessly. There was no hiding it now. I was wearing a poor imitation of the real thing.

Thankfully, the game was exciting, and no one ever noticed a thing. I had dodged a major bullet that day. If my friends had found out, I would have never been able to live that down.

You're probably wondering where the spiritual parallel is, right? Well, the heat from the gymnasium that day revealed what kind of shoes I had. The same is true of the Christian life. Sooner or later God reveals who His people really are. In the case of Ezekiel, God needed to pull the covers off a group of hucksters who were leading the people into destruction.

They were "prophets," or so they said. But there was something fishy about what they said. They always said what the people wanted to hear. Now, who doesn't like someone who always agrees with your point of view, always predicting good things? There's something to be said for having a friend or two who gush about you.

But let's be real—that gets old after a while, especially when their prophetic utterances cloud your view of reality. God too gets tired of those who speak words that lead people to destruction.

139

CAN YOU HEAR ME NOW?

The false prophets of Judah formed a cheering section for the sins of Israel. They justified the wrong that the people were doing, and their justifications often led to the deaths of righteous men and women who spoke out against their wrongs.

God got so angry that He declared through Ezekiel that He would set His face against them: "Because of your false words and lying visions, I am against you, declares the Sovereign Lord. My hand will be against the prophets who see false visions and utter lying divinations" (Ezekiel 13:8, 9). Imagine having God for an enemy!

The soft affirming words of the false prophets of Judah were a cancer, slowly destroying the spirituality of the nation. These verbal assassins spoke words that sounded good. They were down with whatever was happening. Wherever there was a good time to be had, they had it. They heard nothing from God, yet they were quick to share "messages" from Him.

The word of God needs no embellishment or embellishers. If someone claims to have a message from God for you, ask God to confirm it, to make it clear to you. Usually He will, and usually it will be in several different ways.

THE 411. . . . .

Read Ezekiel 13:8-23. Did you notice the way that Ezekiel shared God's words, as if He were in a room nearby? What does this tell you about how God communicates with His people?

Why not ask God to talk to and through you as He did Ezekiel?

Blessings and Curses

"They have left the straight way and wandered off to follow the way of Balaam son of Beor, who loved the wages of wickedness" (2 Peter 2:15).

What would you do for a Klondike bar? If you're older than 25, you no doubt have seen those once-famous commercials in which otherwise upstanding people make a range of animal sounds for the chocolate-coated ice-cream bar.

Let's adjust the Klondike question a bit to say, What would you do for $50,000? What would you be willing to do for a $1 million? Those questions are being answered by the crazy people who sign up to be contestants on the popular reality show *Fear Factor*.

From time to time I've watched in horror as people eat worms, cock-

140

Verbal Assassins

roaches, and other unmentionables, jump from helicopters, etc. On one particularly memorable episode the contestants were asked to eat reindeer testicles and drink 100-year-old eggnog (who knows where they got the eggnog). However, even grosser is the fact that all of them completed the feat, and they did so for a measly $50,000.

Greed is a great motivator to those who don't know God. But let's not be too hard on them. Even those who know the power of God sometimes find themselves doing the unpardonable for the sake of a little extra cheese. Ever watch the unique brand of "gospel" being preached by televangelists today? It's basically designed to pry open wallets and pocketbooks.

But long before today's shady dealers, there was the forerunner of them all, the man who tried to figure out a way to wring more money out of his unique spiritual gifts.

The story begins as Israel makes its way to the Promised Land. On the way the Israelites encounter hostile nations, and one by one they dispose of them, some of whom outnumber them and possess far superior weaponry.

They had just taken care of the Amorites when Moab loomed ahead. The Moabites were terrified of Israel's military prowess and their God. In fact, they knew they didn't really have a chance, so it was with some trepidation that Balak, king of Moab, hatched a desperate plan. He called upon a man known for having strong spiritual powers. It was a long shot, but Balak was desperate.

"A people has come out of Egypt; they cover the face of the land and have settled next to me. Now come and put a curse on these people, because they are too powerful for me. Perhaps then I will be able to defeat them and drive them out of the country. For I know that those you bless are blessed, and those you curse are cursed" (Numbers 22:5, 6).

Balaam, the sorcerer, instantly knew that Balak's request was problematic. Israel was no heathen nation. Their God was the God with the capital G in His name. He was not *a* god; He was *the* God. Cursing Israel was impossible. But Balak wouldn't take no for an answer.

After much trying, Balak managed to get Balaam out to the curse site, only to see Balaam bless Israel. Perhaps if they tried another place and built more altars and performed more sacrifices, God would change His mind and allow Balaam to curse Israel, Balak reasoned. Again, he was wrong. Balak switched sites one more time, and a third time nothing but blessings proceeded from the mouth of Balaam.

Disgusted, Balak decided that he wouldn't give any money to Balaam. "Then Balak's anger burned against Balaam. He struck his hands together

CAN YOU HEAR ME NOW?

and said to him, 'I summoned you to curse my enemies, but you have blessed them these three times. Now leave at once and go home! I said I would reward you handsomely, but the Lord has kept you from being rewarded'" (Numbers 24:10, 11).

The story of Balaam is interesting because of Balaam's behavior. He so desperately craved the money that Balak offered that he openly disrespected God. Balaam knew that he would never be able to curse the Israelites. He even admitted this to Balak's men (Numbers 22:8-20). Balaam was looking for some way to get the money and avoid cursing Israel, even after he was almost killed by an angel (verses 21-35).

Sometimes, like Balaam, we are tempted to sacrifice our integrity for monetary gain. Sometimes there's no money involved at all. Perhaps a carefully chosen word would win us the guy or girl we want or the dream job we want. If it's not what God wants us to do, the best thing to do is leave it alone.

Who knows, the life we save by obeying God may be our own.

THE 411. . . . .

Before Balaam left Balak, he read Moab's future and shared with Balak what was to come. Read Numbers 24:14-25. Why did God allow Himself to be associated with a known sorcerer like Balaam?

Kill Amos!

"Amos is raising a conspiracy against you in the very heart of Israel. The land cannot bear all his words" (Amos 7:10).

Nobody likes a liar. Do you know of anyone who enjoys being around people adept at bearing false witness? Probably not.

Most of us can deal with people who lie about us, providing no bodily harm is done. Sometimes our reputations may suffer a bit, but most of us will endure this humiliation rather than confronting the untruth and its author. At any rate, it's hurtful, and not something we tolerate very often.

If the lies being told about us, however, had the potential to end our lives, that might elicit a more determined response. I've heard it said that "all a person is is their reputation." Whether that's true or not, a good reputation takes time to build, and it is priceless.

Imagine how Amos must have felt when he found out that Amaziah, the high priest from Bethel, was badmouthing him to Jeroboam, king of

142

Verbal Assassins

Israel. Amaziah, for all his ranting and raving, was no closer to God than Satan is. He was a "bought" preacher willing to say only what pleased the evil Jeroboam.

When Amos, a shepherd and dresser of fig trees, showed up from the country to proclaim God's impending judgment, Amaziah sort of laughed him off. He didn't really think Amos was a threat to his religious monopoly. He was wrong.

Amos was persistent, telling his message to anyone who would listen. Soon the people were in an uproar, and Amaziah could no longer overlook the little country preacher who had no religious pedigree.

We pick up the story in Amos 7:10, where a showdown has been convened before the king. The scene is worthy of CNN.

"Then Amaziah the priest of Bethel sent a message to Jeroboam king of Israel: 'Amos is raising a conspiracy against you in the very heart of Israel. The land cannot bear all his words. For this is what Amos is saying: "Jeroboam will die by the sword, and Israel will surely go into exile, away from their native land."'"

Amos must have been really giving Amaziah "the business." Notice how Amaziah throws the king's name into the mix. He knew that anyone who threatened to undermine or overthrow the king could be accused of treason and thereby put to death. Amaziah basically went for the juggler. He leveled the most damaging charge against Amos that he could.

"Then Amaziah said to Amos, 'Get out, you seer! Go back to the land of Judah. Earn your bread there and do your prophesying there. Don't prophesy anymore at Bethel, because this is the king's sanctuary and the temple of the kingdom'" (verses 12, 13).

Amaziah's words were incredibly jarring, especially the last few lines. Not only did he accuse Amos of being a false prophet (or worse, a psychic), but there was in them no mention of God as the unseen head of the temple and the kingdom. That in microcosm was an example of how far Israel had fallen.

Perhaps he reasoned that no one would dare continue defiantly prophesying Israel's doom, certainly not in front of the king. Wrong again. Amos was undaunted.

"Amos answered Amaziah, 'I was neither a prophet nor a prophet's son, but I was a shepherd, and I also took care of sycamore-fig trees. But the Lord took me from tending the flock and said to me, "Go, prophesy to my people Israel."

"'Now then, hear the word of the Lord. You say, "Do not prophesy

143

CAN YOU HEAR ME NOW?

against Israel, and stop preaching against the house of Isaac."

" 'Therefore this is what the Lord says: "Your wife will become a prostitute in the city, and your sons and daughters will fall by the sword. Your land will be measured and divided up, and you yourself will die in a pagan country.

" ' "And Israel will certainly go into exile, away from their native land" ' " (verses 14–17).

Wow! Amos' rebuke of Amaziah is so piercing, so personal, so damning, that the entire royal court must have fallen silent. Amos minced no words. He had a message from God to give, and he gave it. Sadly, Amos was right. Israel's impending captivity would come later.

Amaziah thought he had said the magic words that would forever silence Amos. Boy, was he wrong! God was with Amos, and God plus anyone equals a majority. Amaziah and Israel found that out the hard way.

THE 411. . . . .

What would you have done if you were Amos? Those who remain faithful to God will be called before similar tribunals. Read Matthew 10:1-20 to find out what God has promised to do to help us.

Ask God to help you stand firm when your trial comes.

Stop Hatin'

"On the next Sabbath almost the whole city gathered to hear the word of the Lord" (Acts 13:44).

Jealousy kills. It knows no sex, race, or class. It grows in any soil in which it is planted. There is no level of society that it cannot penetrate. From the street to the ivory tower, from the pew to the pulpit, if you look closely you can see it.

The place it should not be found is the church. If there ever was a place where people should be able to overcome feelings of envy and jealousy, it ought to be the church, right? Yet one occasionally hears of members who wheel and deal to get positions in the church. I once knew someone who tried to rig the work of a church nominating committee. The grand prize of their great effort, you ask? Chair of the church's building committee. Sounds like more trouble than it's worth.

Lest you think men and women of the cloth are exempt from a little political infighting in the name of getting a higher office, think again. In a

144

Verbal Assassins

fraternity in which a plum pastorate at a big church means one has arrived, some are willing to sell their souls to get there.

Some church leaders jealously guard their flock, as well they should. Satan is always looking for ways to break the church. But why erect barriers that block those who are trying to help the church, such as a friend of mine who promotes healthful eating habits and diet reform? One day he shared with me how difficult it is to get into some churches to share this message.

"I run into to all kinds of obstacles. Many people feel threatened by what I have to share, even though they know it to be true and helpful to their congregations," he adds. "It's almost as if they're afraid I'll steal their congregations."

The same was true during the days of the early Christian church. The apostle Paul and Barnabas were cutting a hurricane-size path through the then-Christian world. Fresh off his conversion, Paul spoke powerfully in the Jewish synagogue in Antioch.

He spoke of how God had cared for Abraham and his descendants. He spoke of the preaching of John the Baptist, who prepared the way for Jesus' ministry. He spoke of the power of Jesus' death and resurrection. He closed the message that Sabbath with a bang.

"Therefore, my brothers, I want you to know that through Jesus the forgiveness of sins is proclaimed to you. Through him everyone who believes is justified from everything you could not be justified from by the law of Moses" (Acts 13:38, 39).

Paul's good news was like fresh water to the parched souls of many Jews and Gentiles who had grown accustomed to weak preaching and even weaker living. When he finished, many of the devout Jews followed him and asked him to preach another sermon the next Sabbath. Paul and Barnabas agreed to return.

The next week the synagogue was filled to the gills. Almost the whole city came out to hear them, thanks in no small part to the fact that some of them recognized him as Saul, the Roman enforcer who hunted the Jews. As they preached, however, they noticed that some of the leaders were not exactly saying amen.

They began whispering and plotting against Paul and Barnabas. The more the Jewish elders looked around at the crowd, the more jealous they became of Paul and Barnabas. "When the Jews saw the crowds," Paul writes, "they were filled with jealousy and talked abusively against what Paul was saying" (verse 45).

Paul and Barnabas were quick to answer their verbal assaults. "Then

Can You Hear Me Now?

Paul and Barnabas answered them boldly: 'We had to speak the word of God to you first. Since you reject it and do not consider yourselves worthy of eternal life, we now turn to the Gentiles. For this is what the Lord has commanded us: "I have made you a light for the Gentiles, that you may bring salvation to the ends of the earth"'" (verses 46, 47).

The Gentiles, unbelievers, responded enthusiastically to Paul's offering of salvation, but the Jewish leaders were unconverted. They saw Paul as a threat. From this moment in Antioch, Paul's ministry would be dogged by the infectious whispers of the leaders of that day. No matter where he traveled to preach the gospel, the Jews in that area would disdain his message.

In spite of this, Paul continued his ministry. The lesson to you and me is a simple one. Whenever we try to do God's business, whenever we try to share the message of our soon-coming Savior with a dying world, we will run into problems. Satan will make sure of it. But we are not to be discouraged. God will make a way for us to continue to minister for Him.

The 411. . . . .

Read the rest of the story in Acts 13:46-52. Then get a piece of paper and a pencil. Write a paragraph to complete the following statement: "I choose to share the good news about Jesus because . . ."

The Rule of Love

"Speak and act like people who will be judged by the law that sets us free" (James 2:12, CEV).

Perhaps you have donned the vestments of a verbal assassin sometimes. I know I have. My words are not always flavored with grace. Quite often, the people we feel we can attack with impunity are those who can't fight back, those who either lack the energy or have the good sense not to repay evil for evil.

Those of us who would let our words fly without any thought should heed the counsel of the apostle James. He wrote about a standard by which we will all be judged, not only for what we say but also for what our actions say about us. That's quite a high standard, friend. Here's James's words of caution, as rendered in *The Message:*

"My dear friends, don't let public opinion influence how you live out our glorious, Christ-originated faith. If a man enters your church wearing an expensive suit, and a street person wearing rags comes in right after him,

Verbal Assassins

and you say to the man in the suit, 'Sit here, sir; this is the best seat in the house!' and either ignore the street person or say, 'Better sit here in the back row,' haven't you segregated God's children and proved that you are judges who can't be trusted?

"Listen, dear friends. Isn't it clear by now that God operates quite differently? He chose the world's down-and-out as the kingdom's first citizens, with full rights and privileges. This kingdom is promised to anyone who loves God. And here you are abusing these same citizens! Isn't it the high and mighty who exploit you, who use the courts to rob you blind? Aren't they the ones who scorn the new name—"Christian"—used in your baptisms?

"You do well when you complete the Royal Rule of the Scriptures: 'Love others as you love yourself.' But if you play up to these so-called important people, you go against the rule and stand convicted by it. You can't pick and choose in these things, specializing in keeping one or two things in God's law and ignoring others. The same God who said, 'Don't commit adultery,' also said, 'Don't murder.' If you don't commit adultery but go ahead and murder, do you think your nonadultery will cancel out your murder? No, you're a murderer, period.

"Talk and act like a person expecting to be judged by the Rule that sets us free. For if you refuse to act kindly, you can hardly expect to be treated kindly. Kind mercy wins over harsh judgment every time" (James 2:1-13).

God takes our words very seriously. One day we will be asked to explain what we meant when we said this or that, or when we acted this way or that way. But if we heed James's warning, we need not worry. Before we speak, it would help to put ourselves in the shoes of the one to whom we are speaking. If we exercised this little principle, how many careless words would go unspoken?

THE 411. . . . .

Think back over the past few days. Did you say something to someone that you wished you could retract? Did someone hurt you with their words? How might you make these situations right?

CHAPTER 11

In God's Presence

Behind the Words

"They asked each other, 'Were not our hearts burning within us while he talked with us on the road and opened the Scriptures to us?'" (Luke 24:32).

I love talking with Mr. Brown. That name means nothing to you. "Who is Mr. Brown?" you ask. He's one of my neighbors. He's 70-ish, a dapper dresser, and just the nicest neighbor anyone can have. He and his wife are two treasures in my life. They are special.

Mr. Brown watches our home when we're away. He has also been known to cut my grass when I'm gone on a long trip. When we first moved to Philadelphia, he and his wife made sure we knew what day the trash collectors came, where to park our cars to avoid accidents, who our neighbors were, and how long they had been living in the neighborhood.

All of that is great information, essential stuff I need to know, but I like Mr. Brown for another reason. I like the talks we have.

Recently I ran into him as I returned home from a long trip. I was eager to get in the house and unwind, but the sight of Mr. Brown relaxed me. I knew I was home again.

"Hey, Dwain!" he greeted me enthusiastically. I shook his hand and hugged him.

He is pure grandfather material.

"How are you, Mr. Brown?" I asked.

"Dwain, I can't complain. It wouldn't do any good if I did." It's this kind of statement that draws me to Mr. Brown. He wasn't done dropping pearls of wisdom on this cool September night.

148

In God's Presence

Taking a cue from him, I added, "You know you're right. There's no need to fret when we know that God is in control of everything."

"That's right, Dwain. You know," he intoned, "we didn't bring anything into this world when we came, and we can't take anything with us when we leave."

"This house," he pointed at his home, which sits next to ours, "is not mine. I'm just holding on to it for a while."

I stood listening to Mr. Brown talk about the importance of knowing that God is in charge of everything and that we are just stewards of His gifts. As we parted, he left me with this zinger: "Dwain, I just want to live right. I want to leave a good mark."

His words pierced me deeply. They were not new. They were not profound in and of themselves. People say those words all the time. I've said them, and when I do I hope they come out the way Mr. Brown's did, with meaning and conviction.

What made Mr. Brown's words meaningful was Mr. Brown. He is a person of integrity, a man who fought during the civil rights movement for freedoms I take for granted, a man who served his country in the hell that is war, a man of experience and honor. His life drove home the truth of his words.

The Sunday after Jesus' crucifixion, the news of His resurrection spread throughout the countryside. Luke 24 recounts the story of Jesus' miraculous appearance to two of His disciples as they walked the road to the town of Emmaus. They did not recognize Him.

As the noble Stranger walked with them, they told Him of the fearful crucifixion of the prophet Jesus from Nazareth. "We had hoped that he was the one who was going to redeem Israel," they said (verse 21).

The Stranger responded with surprise. "Did not the Christ have to suffer these things and then enter his glory?" (verse 26). Then He whipped out a scroll of Scriptures and gave them a Bible study on the coming of the Messiah, His death, and resurrection. As they listened they got happier. Everything now made sense. This was all part of the plan.

Later as they ate together, their eyes were opened, and they recognized Jesus. A huge grin broke out on their faces, and they grabbed each other and pointed at Jesus. Almost immediately Jesus disappeared from their presence.

Now it all made sense. He was alive. As they reminisced about their time with the Stranger, they couldn't stop expressing how great it was to be in His presence: "Wasn't it great to talk with Him? My heart skipped a

CAN YOU HEAR ME NOW?

beat when He began to break down the Word to us. You know, I really miss talking with Him" (see verse 32).

THE 411. . . . .
Read the rest of Luke 24. Does anything strike you about God's interaction with His disciples as He prepared to leave them? I am struck by the extent to which Jesus went to assure the disciples that He was with them. Why was this so important?

A Good Scream

"Oh, that you would rend the heavens and come down, that the mountains would tremble before you!" (Isaiah 64:1).

Ever felt as if the presence of God has left you? As if your life is a wasteland of missed opportunities and failures? You look in the mirror, and you want to kill the person staring back at you?

Be honest. You've probably been there a time or two.

When I get to that point, I feel like screaming. To people who don't really know me, I appear relatively calm, easygoing, a somewhat quiet person. My wife would probably beg to differ, and so would her rapidly deteriorating eardrums. I have been known to let out bloodcurdling yells when I feel overwhelmed. It usually scares her to death, but I sure feel better after a good squeal. (Maybe I should try one now! Maybe not.)

I usually feel this way when I'm not really studying God's Word or seeking Him earnestly in prayer. This neglect of my personal devotional life usually causes my sins to metastasize and grow out of control. You know what comes next—a mountain of guilt!

The apostle Paul, one of my favorite Bible characters, asked the following important questions: "What shall we say, then? Shall we go on sinning so that grace may increase? By no means! We died to sin; how can we live in it any longer? Or don't you know that all of us who were baptized into Christ Jesus were baptized into his death? We were therefore buried with him through baptism into death in order that, just as Christ was raised from the dead through the glory of the Father, we too may live a new life" (Romans 6:1-4).

At times when I have not been, or done, all that God expects of me, I wonder out loud if I have really died to sin. Don't you? If my desire is not to make God the laughingstock of the universe, not to shame Him or

150

In God's Presence

allow Him to be ridiculed by the devil, what explains my many falls?

Over time I am learning that being buried with Christ is a daily process. I cannot take two weeks, two days, or two moments off. Each temptation brings with it a fresh opportunity to go to the cross and die with Jesus. In a real sense, every time I choose to do God's will, each time I choose to follow what I know to be right, I crucify the old Dwain so that the new Dwain can live.

When the battle raging inside me—should I or shouldn't I?—gets really out of control, that's when I want to scream with Isaiah: "Rip the heavens apart! Come down, Lord" (Isaiah 64:1, CEV). "Tear the enemy of my soul to bits!"

Those were Isaiah's feelings as he watched the heathen nations of Assyria and Babylon run roughshod over Israel and Judah. These two evil nations were God's chosen enforcers to punish His people for their sins. Isaiah was a prophet to the nation of Judah. God gave him the task of showing Judah their sin. And he didn't bite his tongue.

In Isaiah 1:4 he quotes God's angry words: "Israel, you are a sinful nation loaded down with guilt. You are wicked and corrupt and have turned from the Lord, the holy God of Israel" (CEV). Now, that's what I call a serious tongue-lashing. God is not pleased!

At times Isaiah yearned for God to come down and save His people from the hand of their oppressors. He endured the sight of Assyrian occupation for more than three decades. It was enough to make a grown man scream.

But God did not leave Isaiah and Judah hopeless. He promised them a new beginning, a new place where they would be happy in His presence and He would once again be their God: "I am creating new heavens and a new earth; everything of the past will be forgotten; Celebrate and be glad forever! I am creating a Jerusalem, full of happy people. I will celebrate with Jerusalem and all of its people; there will be no more crying or sorrow in that city" (Isaiah 65:17-19, CEV).

That too deserves a good scream: "YEEEEEEEEESSSSSSSSSSSSSSS!"

THE 411. . . . .

A close friend of yours is feeling really down. They are tired of living, and they have even entertained thoughts of suicide. What would you say to them? How would you help them?

151

CAN YOU HEAR ME NOW?

Never Alone

"I am with you and will watch over you wherever you go, and I will bring you back to this land. I will not leave you until I have done what I have promised you" (Genesis 28:15).

Loneliness. Who likes to be alone? No one. Sure, there are times you need room to breathe, a quiet place to think, to be at rest. That's understandable and very vital to your sanity. A little solitude can do a great deal, but it scares some people. If they ever stop to look at who they are or what they have become, they may not be able to bear the sight.

Loneliness is a great killer. Consider the husband who loses his wife of 43 years of marriage. I had the chance to talk with a visitor who attended my church one Sabbath. He was a neatly dressed older man with kind eyes and a warm spirit. I greeted him and introduced myself. We had barely broached a conversation when he began telling me about his wife.

"My wife was a beautiful woman," he began, "and not just physically. She was a beautiful person. She was the best." His eyes were brimming with affection.

By now he spoke in almost a stream-of-consciousness mode, sharing thoughts of her as they came to his mind. His love for her fell down in torrents of praise. For a moment I wasn't there. He was with her again.

"I lost her three years ago, and life has never been the same. She was the love of my life."

Right then my wife walked up and hugged me. I squeezed her a little tighter than I normally would. I introduced Kemba to him, and he told us what a nice couple we were. He spoke some more about his wife and the great years they had had together, as we hung on every word. At that moment I wished I were God, so that I could raise her from the dead and put her in the arms of her lover again. Theirs was a love nourished through years of hardship, trial, and sacrifice.

Now my new friend was alone, and the pathway of his life seemed a little darker without the one who brightened his days. I couldn't help wondering if he would live much longer. His heart seemed so broken.

Then I thought, *What if he didn't know God? What if he didn't know that God is holding his hand through this dark patch in his journey?* The loneliness we face from day to day is made easier when we know that God is with us, that He cares for us, that no matter how dark things get, no matter who forsakes us, no matter what comes our way, God never leaves us alone. There is assurance in His presence.

In God's Presence

That's what Jacob needed that night in the desert. He knew the fierce wrath of Esau, and he knew he deserved punishment for stealing his brother's birthright (Genesis 28). God poured healing words on his troubled mind. God told him that his descendants would inhabit the land where he was now lying (Genesis 28:13, 14). After hearing those words from God, Jacob probably did a dance in his dreams. *I guess that means I'm not going to die at the hand of Esau,* he no doubt thought.

But God didn't stop there. He went on to say the words that have comforted lonely sinners down through the ages: "I am with you." God wants to be with us. He gets even more excited when we acknowledge His presence by the way we live and the right choices we make.

There isn't a more comforting phrase in the Bible. Why? Because if you have God with you, you have everything you will ever need.

THE 411 . . . .

If you were physically in God's presence right now, what would you say to Him? Did you know that you are in His presence right now? I dare you to tell Him what's on your heart!

Submission

"Submit yourselves, then, to God" (James 4:7).

Have you ever been in a place in which you felt very strange, as if perhaps another spirit or power was in the room? At times you may have visited someone's home or gone into a store, only to feel as if there were some other being in your midst.

My father once told me of an experience he and my mother had when they were visiting the home of a friend. He felt uncomfortable from the moment he got there. It doesn't help that my father is a finicky eater, and doesn't take to other people's cooking very well. He was already uncomfortable as he reminisced about the comforts of home. But something else was wrong.

From the moment he entered the room where they were staying, he felt as if an "evil" spirit were present. He tried to forget about it. He chalked it up to a bad case of jet lag working on his nerves. But no matter how hard he tried, he simply couldn't get comfortable.

At night he would wake up in cold sweats, his pores standing on edge. After a few midnight episodes and my mother's worries about what was

153

CAN YOU HEAR ME NOW?

happening to her husband, my father decided to open God's Word, to call on the name of Jesus. *Surely the name of Jesus ought to clear the room of any devilish spirits,* he thought. The peace he looked for did not come right away, but as he persisted, a sense of calm came over him, and he was able to rest.

I think I have some idea of how my father must have felt. Once, while visiting my wife's family in Los Angeles, California, we took a trek to Venice Beach. If you've ever been there, you've no doubt seen the "crazies" who rule the sidewalks. There are also countless others pressed tightly together along the beach's walk. Vendors hock everything from T-shirts to luggage. Everything and just about anything is for sale.

I remember walking into one of those shops, one that had weird occult paintings and other paraphernalia. I didn't notice what the store sold before I got in there, but it didn't take me long to find out. What I saw made me uncomfortable, but what I felt was even worse. For a moment I felt as if I had descended into a dark place, and this while the southern California sun beamed brightly.

The air was thick with an offensive spirit. I just didn't feel comfortable, and neither did my wife, so we got out of there as fast as we could.

I believe that the presence of God in us wars against the presence of the enemy in us and around us. I believe that God's Holy Spirit makes us aware of the presence of evil, and often He shepherds us safely off of dangerous ground. Most of the time we have absolutely no clue what spiritual battles are ranging around us, or just how much we need God's protection.

We should ever be thankful for the promise that if we submit ourselves to God, His presence comes in the form of His Holy Spirit. And the Bible declares: "Now the Lord is the Spirit; and where the Spirit of the Lord is, there is freedom" (2 Corinthians 3:17).

Our first responsibility in the battle with evil is to submit ourselves to God so that His presence may abide with us and give us peace.

THE 411 . . . .

Read Hebrews 2:14 and 15. What does this scripture say to you about what Jesus accomplished with His life, death, and resurrection?

In God's Presence

Resist

"Resist the devil, and he will flee from you" (James 4:7).

Chris Thompson.

You don't know him, so stop scratching your brain. (Actually, a few of you do know him.) I met Chris during my junior year in high school. It was my first year at Pine Forge Academy. It was his third year.

I can't quite remember how we met, but we quickly became good friends. We both shared a love for quartet music. Chris has one of the most remarkable first tenor voices you'll ever hear, and an even better spirit. We lost track of each other for a while after we graduated. But we reconnected when I moved to Philadelphia a few years ago.

Almost immediately we teleported back to our high school days when we whooped it up in the gym, sang in the academy choir, and fought off the seniors during the junior/senior rumble. The latter memory makes me smile for several reasons. Let me explain.

Chris is a short person, who is pretty unassuming. If he walked into a room, you might miss him, except for the fact that he is a sharp dresser and a genuinely nice person. His size is never an issue with him. He is self-assured and comfortable in his skin. He has presence.

That said, he's one of the guys you'd never want to "mess" with. However, because of his diminutive stature, people are tempted to walk over him. They do so at their own peril, because great men also come in small packages.

In high school I remember watching Chris take on guys who were almost twice his size and hold his own. If ever the juniors had a "beef" with the seniors, Chris was right there, ready to stand up for his brothers. He was not a huge muscular guy; he was short, compact, wiry, and fierce. While others would hesitate at the sight of the seniors, Chris would bring everything he had into the fight. That's what made him a feared opponent. It was this toughness that allowed him to survive the rigors of becoming a marine. Trying to step on Chris is like trying to step on a scorpion. You better pray you get him first.

In the battle with evil, we often do not bring everything we have into the fight. If one were to look at our effort, they might conclude that all is well with us. Truth is, we are battling a fearsome enemy bent on our destruction. But unlike Chris, my brother in arms, we don't maximize our resources.

The Bible is clear about the way our adversary comes to the battle. He pulls no punches: "Be self-controlled and alert. Your enemy the devil

155

CAN YOU HEAR ME NOW?

prowls around like a roaring lion looking for someone to devour" (1 Peter 5:8). The very next verse tells us what to do: "Resist him, standing firm in the faith, because you know that your brothers throughout the world are undergoing the same kind of sufferings" (verse 9).

Peter seems to intimate that when you hold your position and resist the enemy, you strengthen others who are also standing firm. But even more than that, when you resist the promptings and temptations of Satan, he runs from you. Now, does he stay away forever? No. He returns, tempting us to fall again. So we have to do what we know works: We have to ask God for power to stand firm and resist Satan. God has already supplied all the power we need.

The question is: Do we want to resist with every fiber of our being?

THE 411. . . . .

What's your strategy for overcoming the sins that seem to bind you? Do you have one? Read Philippians 4:1-9. Using what you learn from this passage, ask God to show you how to make practical changes in the way you live your life to strengthen your stand for Him.

Draw Near

"Do not be anxious about anything, but in everything, by prayer and petition, with thanksgiving, present your requests to God" (Philippians 4:6).

I've always loved the writings of Ellen G. White. I found this little gem during an especially dark period in my life. She wrote it in the *Review and Herald* of December 3, 1889: "The soul that loves God loves to draw strength from Him by constant communion with Him. When it becomes the habit of the soul to converse with God, the power of the evil one is broken; for Satan cannot abide near the soul that draws nigh unto God."

Isn't that a great thought? Think about it for a moment. God is the great "anti-Satan." Wherever He is, Satan has to leave. He must bring some kind of sin repellent, because the enemy has to flee at His presence.

White's terrific quotation reminds me of the story of the demon-possessed man who ran naked among the tombs in the region of Gadara. As Jesus and the disciples anchored their boat and began to come ashore, a "freakish"-looking guy bolted toward them. Immediately the disciples scattered. Jesus, however, was unmoved. As the man approached, the terror of his possession left his face hollow and gaunt. Jesus could see that this lost

156

In God's Presence

soul needed help. He heard the unspoken cry of the demonic heart. He knew that this man longed to be delivered. How could He not help him?

When the demonic reached Jesus, he did something very strange. A friend pointed it out to me in Mark 5:6: "But when he [the demonic] saw Jesus afar off, he ran and worshipped him" (KJV). My buddy then asked, "What kind of worship service was that?" I wish I could have been there.

The demons that controlled this poor guy were still subject to the power of Jesus. They could not resist Him. If you read the rest of the story, you will hear them plead for their lives and immediately leave the possessed man at Jesus' command. Wow, what a God!

This story tells an important truth that we all must grasp: In the presence of God there is victory over every sin or demon that threatens us. The demons recognized that they were in the presence of their Creator and that one thought from Him could blot out their existence.

When was the last time you slipped into God's presence? No, I'm not talking about when you were in church, although that's a good place to find Him. What I'm asking is When was the last time you were alone with God, one on one, with no distractions? When was the last time you heard His voice?

James 4:8 says, "Come near to God and he will come near to you." You and I have to learn to crave the presence of God, and not simply because our petitions get answered. That's a great fringe benefit, but would you still yearn for His presence if He decided to close up the gift store in heaven?

Until we get there, we might never really know the joy of hearing God speak.

Get a little closer today. Don't be shy!

THE 411. . . . .
Write God a letter. Tell Him what you think about Him. Don't dwell too much on what you need or want. Just tell Him how much you appreciate Him and why. Share it with a friend if you wish.

Show Me

"Then Moses said, 'Now show me your glory'" (Exodus 33:18).

When words are not enough, why not ask God to show Himself to you? Are you afraid of what you'll see? Read the following passage. Pay special attention to the exchanges between Moses and God.

Can You Hear Me Now?

"Moses said to the Lord, 'You have been telling me, "Lead these people," but you have not let me know whom you will send with me. You have said, "I know you by name and you have found favor with me."

" 'If you are pleased with me, teach me your ways so I may know you and continue to find favor with you. Remember that this nation is your people.'

"The Lord replied, 'My Presence will go with you, and I will give you rest' " (Exodus 33:13, 14).

Imagine if God looked you in the eye and promised to go with you everywhere and to give you rest when you're exhausted. Wow!

God and Moses continue their talk.

"Then Moses said to him, 'If your Presence does not go with us, do not send us up from here. How will anyone know that you are pleased with me and with your people unless you go with us? What else will distinguish me and your people from all the other people on the face of the earth?'

"And the Lord said to Moses, 'I will do the very thing you have asked, because I am pleased with you and I know you by name.'

"Then Moses said, 'Now show me your glory.'

"And the Lord said, 'I will cause all my goodness to pass in front of you, and I will proclaim my name, the Lord, in your presence. I will have mercy, and I will have compassion on whom I will have compassion. But,' he said, 'you cannot see my face, for no one may see me and live.'

"Then the Lord said, 'There is a place near me where you may stand on a rock. When my glory passes by, I will put you in a cleft in the rock and cover you with my hand until I have passed by. Then I will remove my hand and you will see my back; but my face must not be seen' " (verses 15-23).

Didn't you get goose bumps reading that passage from Exodus 33? God really talks, and He doesn't mind doing so face to face. That should quiet all those who claim that they can't see God, hear Him, or touch Him.

What would prompt God to speak with Moses this way? The short answer is that God and Moses were friends. From the time Moses fled Egypt for the school of the wilderness to the time he returned to lead Israel out of bondage, he stayed in constant communication with God. How else can we explain the fact that God seems to "do" what Moses asks? Moses holds God to His word, and God keeps His word. Moses asks, and God answers.

Now, that's cool! That's also exactly what God has in mind for His relationship with you. You too can come close to God. If you do, you will ask what you will, and God will answer.

Believe it.

In God's Presence

THE 411. . . . .

Read Exodus 32 and 33:1-11. What events led to Moses' talk with God? What was God's attitude toward Israel before He talked with Moses? Isn't it refreshing to know that God listens to our pleas and is willing to change His mind?

What do you want God to do for you? It's time you spoke with Him.